The Suffering God

& Comfort
Those
Who Hurt

Charles
Ohlrich

Foreword by Philip Yancey

There is only one means to endure our suffering, and that is to understand His, to hook ours onto His, to remember that ours *is* His.

Louis Evely

The Suffering God

*Hope & Comfort
for Those
Who Hurt*

Charles Ohlrich

Foreword by Philip Yancey

InterVarsity Press
Downers Grove
Illinois 60515

© 1982 by Inter-Varsity Christian Fellowship of the United States of America

All rights reserved. No part of this book may be reproduced in any form
without written permission from InterVarsity Press, Downers Grove, Illinois.

InterVarsity Press is the book-publishing division of Inter-Varsity Christian
Fellowship, a student movement active on campus at hundreds of universities,
colleges and schools of nursing. For information about local and regional
activities, write IVCF, 233 Langdon St., Madison, WI 53703.

Distributed in Canada through InterVarsity Press, 1875 Leslie St., Unit 10,
Don Mills, Ontario M3B 2M5, Canada.

All quotations from Scripture, unless otherwise noted, are from the Holy Bible:
New International Version, copyright © 1978 by the New York Bible Society.
Used by permission of Zondervan Bible Publishers.

Cover photograph: Robert Hayes

ISBN 0-87784-376-7

Printed in the United States of America

Library of Congress Cataloging in Publication Data

Ohlrich, Charles, 1954-
    The suffering God.

    Includes bibliography references.
    1. Suffering of God.   2. Suffering–Religious
aspects–Christianity.   I. Title.
BT153.S8035   231′.8   82-7815
ISBN 0-87784-376-7 (pbk.)   AACR2

15	14	13	12	11	10	9	8	7	6	5	4	3	2	1
94	93	92	91	90	89	88	87	86	85	84	83	82		

For my parents, Charles and Doreas

Acknowledgments

I wish to thank
Carole Sanderson Streeter
for all her help and
encouragement and
Melody Bourland for
typing the manuscript.

Foreword

Many times in my writing career I have found myself interviewing a person who has endured unimaginable pain: cancer, permanent paralysis, leprosy. More than once, those suffering people who have faith in Christ have said something like this to me: "There comes a point when nothing my religion contains helps me. No proposition or explanation affects the pain—just as it didn't with Job. At that moment, I concentrate my mind on Jesus as he hung nailed to a rough cross. I think, 'At least God knows what I feel. He's been there too.' It's not much, but it is something. I don't know how I could survive without the confidence that a loving God does indeed understand my pain."

What those people have expressed to me personally, so often that I think it almost a normative experience for sufferers, I have seldom seen explored theologically. Isn't it strange that an image and a concept that can have such profound effects is so often over-looked in books exploring the character of God? Could it be that we have inherited the deist's tendency to regard God as an impersonal, unchangeable and therefore almost nonexisting being? In the Bible, he is far from that. The recurrent image in the prophets is of a jilted lover, now angry, now tearful, now remorseful, yearning for the renewed love of a fickle people.

Have we lost the profound significance of the fact that God willingly humiliated himself in a scarred and bleeding body? It defies imagination, and yet it is the crux of our faith. Other religions ask humanity to rise above their pain, or perhaps to deny it altogether. In Christianity, we do not rise above our pain; rather, God descends to it.

Chuck Ohlrich points to an aspect of God's character we have grossly overlooked. What he says will worry some people, perhaps rattling their conceptions of God. That, I think, is good. We need a corrective, a fresh look at a theme implicit in Scripture and, in fact, set in motion "before the foundations of the world." Chuck does not say all that could be said about the image of the suffering God, but he points us in the right direction.

Philip Yancey

Preface

This is a book about God. It addresses the question, What is God like, particularly in light of the problem of pain?

As I have written, I have had in mind both seekers and pilgrims—seekers who have moved beyond the question of God's existence to wonder how God's alleged benevolence squares with human anguish, and pilgrims who because of personal suffering have begun to doubt the goodness of God which they once trusted.

Our journey will lead to the cross of Jesus Christ. There and only there will we find a satisfactory answer to the question of God's goodness in light of human suffering. My prayer is that along the way our vision, blurred by confusion, doubt or pain, may be sharpened to view the cross clearly, for it is the discovery of God's nature as revealed in the cross that results in certainty about the goodness of God.

1
The Sufferer's Pursuit of God

Distress over suffering, whether that of others or our own, draws many of us to the book of Job. Job's remarkable appeal lies in its down-to-earth grappling with a universal problem of faith—the problem of pain.

In Job we encounter, not a stained-glass figure, but a very real man who endures trials far beyond those of most; not the superficial piety of the untried, but the authentic piety of an enraged individual who openly gives voice to his inner turmoil. It is gross understatement to say that affliction enters the life of Job or that Job patiently endures the testing of his faith. In Job's case, pain doesn't *enter*—it savagely *assaults*. And it issues not in composed forbearance but in turbulent skepticism. Evil personified repeatedly attacks Job, all but killing him. The result is that his faith in a benevolent creator is shaken to its very foundations.

Those of us who have doubted God are relieved to find in Job someone with whom we can really identify. As we listen to Job cry out to God, we hear ourselves.

The Story of Job

Job's distress began on a day he and his wife were at home while all their children were celebrating at their eldest son's house. In the midst of this joyous occasion, perhaps even as Job thankfully recalled years of family blessing, troubles suddenly overwhelmed him. A messenger burst into his house, announcing the first in a series of calamities: A band of nomads had killed many of his servants and stolen his oxen and donkeys.

Then, while the first was still speaking, a second messenger entered to report that lightning had started a fire which had killed all his sheep and many more servants. A third messenger then entered and reported that a band of Chaldeans had killed still more servants and stolen all his camels. Finally, a fourth man entered, bringing the worst news of all. A violent windstorm had collapsed the home of his eldest son, killing all his children.

Any one of these catastrophes would have been hard to bear, but to face them all at once must have been devastating. Job's mind must have reeled at the impact. Why was all this happening? Had all of the blessings been nothing but a cruel trick? Was divine graciousness really the sinister preparation for divine torture?

But this was not the end of Job's suffering. He had lost wealth, friends and family; he next was stripped of his health. His pain was excruciating—"painful sores from the soles of his feet to the top of his head" (2:7). His body was so severely afflicted that people could barely recognize him.

For seven days and nights he could only lie among ash heaps, unable to speak. Many of us experience loss in one area of our lives; Job experienced simultaneous loss in nearly all areas. Words like *despair* or *anguish* are inadequate to describe what must have taken place in Job's mind.

On the eighth day Job finally spoke his mind as he engaged in a series of long discussions with his three friends—Eliphaz, Bildad and Zophar. (They attribute Job's suffering to his sins, but, as we learn in the end, they are wrong.) For a while Job was so overtaken by the suddenness of the calamities that he could not speak. Now he finds he cannot suppress his feelings:

> *If only my anguish could be weighed*
> *and all my misery be placed on the scales!*
> *It would surely outweigh the sand of the seas–(6:2-3)*

> *Therefore I will not keep silent;*
> *I will speak out in the anguish of my spirit,*

I will complain in the bitterness of my soul. (7:11)

If only I had never come into being,
or had been carried straight from the womb to
the grave! (10:19)

Job is so overwhelmed that he feels drowned in his afflictions. The pain and the grief are so unbearable he wants to die:
Oh, that I might have my request,
that God would grant what I hope for,
that God would be willing to crush me,
to let loose his hand and cut me off! (6:8-9)
Job faces a crisis in meaning:
I despise my life . . .
my days have no meaning. (7:16)
Job perhaps could have faced his trials more steadfastly had his faith in a benevolent God remained sure. But he feels that God has turned on him, that God has abandoned him. It is because his *trust* in God has been shaken that Job feels life has lost all meaning.

In the dialog Job makes two assertions which explain this loss of trust. First, he maintains his innocence (9:21, 13:18). His "friends" accuse him of having sinned, but he repeatedly denies this—not that he believes himself to be sinless, but with respect to his immediate suffering he believes he is undeserving. He sincerely feels he has done nothing to merit his afflictions. At one point he even cries to God, "You know that I am not guilty . . . " (10:7).

At the same time he also affirms God's omniscience and sovereignty. Suffering isn't outside God's awareness, nor is it outside his control, so to some degree God is responsible for it. At the very least he allows it. Taking these two elements together, his innocence and God's responsibility, Job questions God's goodness and loses his former trust in him. Job even feels God directly caused his pain.

Now God himself had not caused Job's pain, and, by the end of his experience, I believe Job came to realize this. The author of Job attributes Job's afflictions to Satan, not God. The idea that every time a person suffers God must be the cause is denied by the book of Job. Because we exist in a *uni*verse, one interrelated world, none of us escapes the effects of the Fall; suffering has entered into and mars all human experience. Suffering is simply part of life.

But what we must come to grips with is that to some extent God is responsible for human suffering in that he allows it. This is the tension in which many sufferers live: on the one hand, they believe in a benevolent Creator; on the other, they are experiencing undeserved pain. Can they continue to believe in a good God in light of their suffering?

The Sufferer's Rejection of God
Of course some people deny the existence of God altogether. In that case there is no tension. But most of us tend to deny the benevolence of God rather than his existence.

In 1960, after four intensely happy years of marriage, C. S. Lewis's wife, Joy, died of cancer. In an effort to assuage his grief and guard himself against losing his faith, Lewis wrote a journal in which he openly expressed his feelings and doubts. A few years later the journal was published under the title *A Grief Observed*. In the early pages, Lewis writes, "Not that I am . . . in much danger of ceasing to believe in God. The real danger is coming to believe such dreadful things about Him. The conclusion I dread is not 'So there's no God after all,' but 'So this is what God's really like. Deceive yourself no longer.' "[1]

In *The Brothers Karamazov* Dostoyevsky's character Ivan expresses the same feeling in a slightly different manner. Ivan tells the story of a child who accidentally hit a dog with a stone while playing. The next day the dog's master has the child torn to pieces before his mother's eyes. Ivan then says, "It's not that I don't accept God, you must understand, it's the world created by Him I don't and cannot accept."[2] Ivan doesn't doubt God's existence, he rejects the idea of his goodness. What he is saying is that since the world mirrors the Deity and the world is evil, the Deity must be evil.

Like Lewis and Ivan Karamazov, Job also faces the grim fact that the evidence of life points to a malevolent life-giver. As Job ponders his innocence and God's responsibility, anger wells up within him. That anger rises to the surface in the dialog. At times Job openly accuses God of being unjust: "though I call for help, there is no justice" (19:7).

It is the character of God and the justness of his

government of the world that is on trial in the book of Job. God appears omnipotent to Job but not just.

More dramatically, Job accuses God of cruelty and sadism:

Even if I summoned him and he responded,
I do not believe he would give me a hearing.
He would crush me with a storm
and multiply my wounds for no reason.
He would not let me regain my breath
but would overwhelm me with misery. . . .
When a scourge brings sudden death,
he mocks the despair of the innocent.
(9:16-18, 23)

God has become an enemy to Job:

God assails me and tears me in his anger
and gnashes his teeth at me;
my opponent fastens on me his piercing eyes.
(16:9)

God is described as the destroyer of hope:

But as a mountain erodes and crumbles
and as a rock is moved from its place,
as water wears away stones
and torrents wash away the soil,
so you destroy man's hope. (14:18-19)

Some of us perhaps are shocked by Job's blatant accusations. We might expect that someone who has spoken this way would be instantly judged. That Job survives to the end of the book may seem a minor miracle! Yet even more shocking is the divine pronouncement in chapter 42 that Job had spoken rightly. Not only does Job evade God's wrath, he

meets with his favor. What possible explanation is
there for this?

God Respects Honesty

In the prologue God describes Job as a man of integrity. The violent expression of anger and doubt which
follows in the dialogs is not a denial of this integrity
but an expression of it. Integrity and honesty go hand
in hand. When undeserved suffering overcomes Job
he has the integrity to face reality and the honesty to
voice his doubts. God respects this honesty above
mindless submission.

As long as a person is not being presumptuous
or opportunistic, it is all right to cry out to God in
angry desperation. This is one of the lessons God
desires us to learn from Job. It is not sinful to tell
God how we feel—even if some of the things we say
may be wrong. If you have experienced great suffering and have found yourself saying things similar
to what Job said, know that God understands this.
Even if you are a Christian and have been shaken
to the point of doubting the whole thing, God still
understands. In my own pilgrimage I have sometimes
slipped back to agnosticism and even atheism. But
when I start to condemn myself, I come back to the
book of Job and remember that God's praise for Job
at the end of the book indicates that "God is more
pleased with daring honesty, even when this involves
doubt about God and His ways with man, than He
is with a superficial attempt to maintain a shallow
creed in the face of shattering evidence."[3]

Job's defiance arises, not from a sinful desire to usurp the throne of God—as his three accusing friends suppose—but from the depth of his sorrow. I believe that in God's providence books such as Job and the Psalms came to be included in the canon because God wishes sufferers to know that he understands their sorrow.

The Paradox of Rejection

Another reason that God praises Job is that there is a deeper significance—in fact, a paradoxical significance—to his fierce replies to God. While it appears that Job is merely rejecting God, in actuality he is drawing near to him, and God knows this. The paradox of Job's rejection of God is that *underneath he still pursues.* Job's quarrel with God is a lover's quarrel. His apparent hate and rejection are born out of desire for affirmation and reconciliation. They merely appear in the guise of hate and rejection. Job is the embodiment of Hosea's description of a penitent Israel: "they will seek my face; in their misery they will earnestly seek me" (5:15).

While I was an undergraduate, I knew a young man who vividly reflected this verse. For over a year he had studied Christianity, sincerely and zealously searching for God. Members of both Campus Crusade and Inter-Varsity had spoken with him at length during this time. It was just after Christmas that he seemed ready to put his faith in Christ.

Then word came of a tragedy in his family. Overnight his seeking after God inverted into intense reviling. He cursed any Christian who attempted to speak with him and raged at God himself. Those who had spent time witnessing to him were dejected. Most of them felt there was no longer any hope for him to become a believer. What had seemed to be an approaching celebration had turned into bitter disappointment.

Two weeks later that young man gave his allegiance to Christ. His friends were stunned! They were very happy, but frankly perplexed. Many were doubtful; they felt his commitment wouldn't last. But it did.

What had happened was that under a smokescreen of reviling, he was drawing even nearer to God in his sorrow. Unfortunately, all his friends could see was the smoke. On the surface such situations may appear hopeless, but in the desperation which affliction can bring about, we must, as it were, read between the lines of the sufferer's words. Most of all we must never be judgmental as Job's three friends were. In spirit a person can be closest to God when verbally he appears to be furthest away. Ironically, Job's three friends exemplify the reverse; they honored God with their lips, but their hearts were far from him.

Job questions God's character but primarily he *probes* it. This probing constitutes the theme of the book of Job. On the surface we may hear Job furiously appealing to God as Judge in order to prove his innocence and thereby condemn God. But as we look deeper into the text we discover that the central arena in the book of Job is not the courtroom but the heart. It is God himself that Job seeks, not just to win his case. Job appeals not only to God as Judge but to God as Father. He wants somehow to find that God is caring despite seeming indifference, that he is good despite apparent malevolence. He desires a revelation of God's nature.

Perhaps it is best stated in this way: Job is hoping for a vision of God as he responds to human suffering. Does God really care about human suffering? How does human anguish affect him? If Job could look on God's face, what would he see? In his anger, Job can only picture God as far removed in the vaulted heavens with either no expression on his face or with an expression of sadistic enjoyment.

The pathos of Job's search is heard in his question, "Does it please you to oppress me?" (10:3). Job desperately wants to hear the answer no and to see a vision of a caring face, but as yet, in his agony, he sees nothing but a void. "Why do you hide your face?" he cries (13:24).

What Job seeks, what we seek in our despair, is an unveiling of God's heart, a vision of his face. Seeing God becomes the focus of our desire. In the midst of evil we want to find goodness in God, in the midst of ugliness we long for a vision of beauty in God, and by means of this discovery and this vision we want to transcend the evil and ugliness which engulfs us:

One thing I ask of the LORD,
*   this is what I seek:*
that I may dwell in the house of the LORD

> *all the days of my life,*
> *to gaze upon the beauty of the* LORD
> *and to seek him in his temple. . . .*
> *Then my head will be exalted*
> *above the enemies who surround me. . . .*
> *My heart says of you, "Seek his face!"*
> *Your face,* LORD, *I will seek.*
> *Do not hide your face from me. . . .*
> *I am still confident of this:*
> *I will see the goodness of the* LORD
> *in the land of the living. (Ps 27:4, 6, 8-9, 13)*

This is what Job desired and this is what we desire—
to see God.

And the exciting message of the Bible is that when
we have this desire, God responds. At the end of the
book of Job God appears before Job and reveals himself. Job exclaims:

> *Surely I spoke of things I did not understand,*
> *things too wonderful for me to know. . . .*
> *My ears had heard of you*
> *but now my eyes have seen you.*
> *Therefore I despise myself*
> *and repent in dust and ashes. (Job 42:3, 5-6)*

Job is completely turned around as the Lord opens
his heart to him. God grants to Job an intimate knowledge of himself, that he should find strength in this
knowledge—"the people that know their God shall be
strong" (Dan 11:32 KJV)—and that he should find
comfort in this knowledge—"for knowing God is a
relationship calculated to thrill a man's heart."[4] He
desires the same for you and for me.

Jesus Christ: The Focus of God's Self-Revelation

For Job the search for God led to the appearance of God in nature. For us the search for God must lead to the person of Jesus Christ, God made flesh. Since his appearing all other sources of revelation have become secondary. He is the one and only visible image of the invisible God. All who would know God must come to Christ, "for there is no other name under heaven given to men by which we must be saved" (Acts 4:12). Or, as Luke records Jesus' words, "All things have been committed to me by my Father.... No one knows who the Father is except the Son and those to whom the Son chooses to reveal him" (Lk 10:22).

In the next chapter we will consider the gospel account of the Son of God. Then in subsequent chapters, using both the Old and New Testaments, we will attempt to deepen our understanding of who his Father is. In so doing we will hope to see into the holy of holies, to peer beyond the veil of mystery in search of a love which reaches out to us in our pain, a light that penetrates our darkness, an evidence of divine goodness which supersedes the evidence of divine malevolence.

2

The Messiah and His Cross

Spiritual and political turmoil dominate Jewish history. Until their return from the Babylonian exile, the Jews could easily and rightly blame their misfortunes, as the prophets boldly did, on their own misconduct. Following the exile, however, during the intertestamental period, most Jews began to stress the Law and sincerely tried to obey God's commandments. There were few incidents of idol worship. Yet, rather than becoming prosperous, the Jews continued to pass from one fateful subjection to another.

Their suffering became particularly acute during

the reign of Antiochus IV (175-163 B.C.), who in-
flicted terrible cruelties on them, not stopping short
of mass murder. All this suffering seemed to come
undeserved.

Here we have the Job problem again, the problem
of faith which plagues us all—the suffering of the
innocent. It is one thing when affliction overtakes
an overtly evil person or nation; it is another when
calamity falls on those who least seem to deserve it.
Where is God when this happens? How can we continue to believe that God is good in light of such
injustice?

In the context of the afflictions of the intertestamental period, especially those encountered during
the reign of Antiochus IV, a genre of literature known
as "apocalyptic" flourished among the Jewish people.
These writings were futuristic, intending to show
how God would soon bring mighty victory to his
people, though at the time they were in the midst
of an apparently hopeless situation. God may have as
yet refrained from intervention, but soon he would
emerge on the scene. Israel found comfort and
strength in the hope that God was about to work
out his sovereign purposes despite all the inescapable
perplexities of the moment.

The term *apocalyptic* comes from the Greek word
apokalypsis, which means "an unveiling, disclosure
or revelation." Behind the extravagant symbolism,
exaggerated descriptions of warfare and laborious
numerical calculations found in these writings lies
an underlying yearning for an unveiling of God. It

was this with which the people identified. The Jews desperately needed to sense Jehovah's allegiance and to know his presence, for they felt abandoned by him, just as Job had.

It is therefore not surprising that a recurrent theme in apocalyptic literature has to do with the appearance of a flesh-and-blood personage—the coming Messiah. The Messiah, it was believed, would be a righteous king, like David and descended from him, who would lead Israel to glories they had never known before. He was to be God's special agent in a plan of mighty deliverance.

The Messianic hope centered on the line of David because the memory of David was cherished beyond that of all other kings and the age of his reign in Jerusalem was considered the golden age of Israel:

> He stood out as a bright and shining light for the God of Israel. His accomplishments were many and varied; man of action, poet, tender lover, generous foe, stern dispenser of justice, loyal friend, he was all that men find wholesome and admirable in a man, and this by the will of God, who made him and shaped him for his destiny. It is to David, not to Saul, that Jews look back with pride and affection as the establisher of their kingdom, and it is in David that the more far-sighted of them saw the kingly ideal beyond which their minds could not reach, in the image of which they looked for a coming Messiah, who should deliver his people, and sit upon the throne of David forever. [1]

The expectation of the Davidic Messiah stemmed

from the promise in 2 Samuel: "Your house and your kingdom will endure forever before me; your throne will be established forever" (7:16). Other references to the Messiah in the Old Testament are many:

> For to us a child is born,
>   to us a son is given,
>   and the government will be on his shoulders.
> And he will be called
>   Wonderful Counselor, Mighty God,
>   Everlasting Father, Prince of Peace.
> Of the increase of his government and peace
>   there will be no end.
> He will reign on David's throne
>   and over his kingdom,
> establishing and upholding it
>   with justice and righteousness
>   from that time on and forever. (Is 9:6-7)

> "The days are coming," declares the LORD,
>   "when I will raise up to David a righteous Branch,
> a King who will reign wisely
>   and do what is just and right in the land." (Jer 23:5)

> For this is what the LORD says: "David will never fail to have a man to sit on the throne of the house of Israel." (Jer 33:17)

> I will place over them one shepherd, my servant David, and he will tend them; he will tend them and be their shepherd. I the LORD will be their God, and my servant

David will be prince among them. I the LORD *have
spoken. (Ezek 34:23-24)*

Such titles as "son of David" and "the Lord's anointed"
became associated with the advent of this one on
whom the Jews pinned their hopes—the Messiah for
whom they prayed and waited.

The Rise and Fall of Jesus Christ

When Jesus began his ministry, the response of the
public was explosive. Wherever Jesus preached, the
turnout was enormous. In our age, we would have to
look to the excitement and turnout of a Superbowl
to find something comparable. Crowds beyond
numbering flocked to Jesus. Note how Mark describes the crowds: "the whole town gathered at the
door" (1:33); "so many gathered that there was no
room left, not even outside the door" (2:2); "the
crowd that gathered around him was so large that
he got into a boat and sat in it out on the lake" (4:1);
"a large crowd followed and pressed around him"
(5:24); "so many people were coming and going that
they did not even have a chance to eat" (6:31). In
the fourth Gospel, an amazed observer is quoted as
saying, "Look how the whole world has gone after
him!" (Jn 12:19). How are we to account for this
tremendous public response to the son of a carpenter
from the little town of Nazareth?

The reason was that Jesus demonstrated himself
to be the Messiah through his teaching, his power
to heal and perform miracles, and his compassion.

Word quickly spread that he was the one they had

awaited: "All the people were astonished and said,
'Could this be the Son of David?' " (Mt 12:23). "The
first thing Andrew did was to find his brother Simon
and tell him, 'We have found the Messiah' " (Jn 1:41).
"Then, leaving her water jar, the woman went back
to the town and said to the people, 'Come, see a man
who told me everything I ever did. Could this be the
Christ?' " (Jn 4:28-29). Expectation and anticipation
rose in people's hearts as it looked as though the hope
of centuries were being realized.

In one of the towns where Jesus ministered, the
people made the following response which, in light
of the sufferer's pursuit of God, beautifully sums up
the excitement over Jesus: "God has come to help
his people" (Lk 7:16). There is deep pathos and relief
in these words. I imagine there were tears in the eyes
of those who said them. In the presence of Jesus,
an oppressed people felt the presence of God. In en-
countering Jesus, they felt that they encountered the
God who sent him. God finally was doing something.
Finally there was something tangible the people could
reach out to in their sorrow—the Messiah, a flesh-
and-blood person sent by God. And so they listened
to him and followed him. To be near to him was to be
near a God who cared.

As we look further into the Gospel account of Jesus
of Nazareth, we find another trend developing among
the people of Palestine, which is somewhat difficult
to understand. At the same time that Christ's ministry is being widely accepted, a movement in the
opposite direction begins. Rather than being drawn

to Jesus, many of the religious leaders are offended by him. Some are so angered that they plot to kill him. As time passes, even Jesus' closest companions begin to doubt his ministry: "From this time many of his disciples turned back and no longer followed him" (Jn 6:66).

John the Baptist's doubt is particularly astonishing: "When John heard in prison what Christ was doing, he sent his disciples to ask him, 'Are you the one who was to come, or should we expect someone else?" (Mt 11:2-3). John had been the herald of Jesus' Messianic mission. He had seen the dove descend on Jesus and then in effect had said, "Behold your Messiah!" Yet now John questions Jesus' identity. This countermovement of doubt and rejection reaches its apex as Jesus is arrested: "Then all the disciples deserted him and fled" (Mt 26:56).

This rejection is especially hard to understand in light of the fact that Jesus so perfectly fit the description of David quoted earlier: "man of action, poet, tender lover, generous foe, stern dispenser of justice, loyal friend . . . all that men find admirable and wholesome in a man." This was Jesus. Jesus passed the test; he met the highest standards; he fulfilled the nearly impossible qualification of being like David. Even his enemies found him to be a man of righteousness, integrity and goodness.

The key to understanding the rejection of Jesus lies in the tension between what people expected of the Messiah and what they actually found in Jesus. In his ministry, the people saw much of what they expected, but they also saw and heard things which they had not expected. Let us consider one of those things.

The Suffering of the Messiah

Peter's famous confession in Matthew 16:16 (see also Mk 8:29 and Lk 9:20) represents a climax in the ministry of Jesus. It also marks the introduction of an entirely new element in Jesus' teaching—the teaching of his suffering and death. It is from this point that the shadow of the cross falls over the ministry of Jesus:

> From that time on Jesus began to explain to his disciples that he must go to Jerusalem and suffer many things at the hands of the elders, chief priests and teachers of the law, and that he must be killed and on the third day be raised to life. (Mt 16:21)

Jesus' message that all people are sinners was unacceptable to a number of the religious leaders, but the message of the crucifixion was unacceptable to nearly everyone, including the disciples. If Jesus were to suffer and die, all of their hopes for deliverance would be shattered. The suggestion of Jesus' suffering and death was therefore unacceptable to them: "Peter took him aside and began to rebuke him. 'Never, Lord!' he said. 'This shall never happen to you!' " (Mt 16:22).

William Barclay writes of Peter's reaction:

> Of course, it was due to horror at the suggestion that such a fate awaited the Master whom he loved. But it was also due to the fact that he was totally incapable of effecting any possible kind of connection between the Son of Man and suffering and death. The two ideas

belonged to different worlds. To Peter the statement of Jesus was not only heartbreaking; it was completely incredible and utterly impossible. In that moment he was confronted with a teaching which his mind was quite unable to grasp and his reaction was shock and even violent incredulity.[2]

For the disciples and all Jews, the idea of the Messiah was connected with glory, power, majesty, victory; in short, with all that contrasted with their own disadvantaged estate. Now Jesus suggests that the same hardship, deprivation, rejection, suffering and death would fall on him. Imagine the desperation of the disciples! This was the one on whom they had pinned their hopes for release. He was to be their vindicator. How could he suggest that his fate would be much the same as theirs?

To make matters worse, the teaching about his sufferings became Jesus' central teaching. It was often on his lips (Mt 17:12, 22-23; 20:17-19, 28; 21:38; 26:2).

The Jews had had more than their share of suffering. They in a sense felt as though they had been nailed to a Roman cross. But the prophets and apocalyptic writers had stirred within them the hope of the Messianic mission—a mission in which crucified Israel would be revealed in great power. Now Jesus makes the incredible assertion that in the Messianic mission God's power would be revealed in crucifixion.

A few days before his crucifixion, Jesus tells the disciples that his purpose will only be accomplished by his death (Jn 12:23-28). The cross was no afterthought, nor a necessity accepted under the compulsion of unfortunate circumstances. It was Jesus' chosen way: "I lay down my life.... No one takes it from me, but I lay it down of my own accord" (Jn 10:17-18). Jesus came into the world to save sinners, and this by giving his life as a ransom (1 Tim 1:15; Mt 20:28). The cross was the intention, the focus and the meaning of Jesus' Messianic mission. It also was the reason he was abandoned.

The Resurrection and the Messianic Question

Before his death, Jesus predicted his rejection and the disciples' sorrow. But he said that soon they would see him again and that their sorrow would be turned into great joy. The parable of the mustard seed indicated that the same gospel which had been rejected would regain acceptance and from very small beginnings would grow in influence and spread throughout the entire world.

Of course, this is exactly what happened. Why? Because of the resurrection. It was the resurrection which proved Jesus was the Messiah. This was the miracle of miracles. Jesus Christ rose again from the dead. In the resurrection many people found a display of glory and power sufficient to overturn the doubts they had had.

In the preaching of the early church, the resurrection became a focal point. Jesus had triumphed over death and now ruled from heaven. And the excitement of new believers was that the same power which had raised Jesus from the dead was working within them, waging a victorious war against sin.

But how would Jesus' sufferings be interpreted? What does a suffering Messiah reveal about the nature of God?

The Doctrine of Impassibility

Unfortunately, the formal theological tradition which developed within the early church, as reflected especially in the ante-Nicene and early post-Nicene era (ca A.D. 150-450), was heavily influenced by Greek philosophy. Thus much thought about a suffering Messiah was short-circuited by Greek philosophical assumptions about the nature of God—in particular, his impassibility. The term *impassible* means "incapable of suffering." For the most part, these early theologians simply carried over Plato's argument that the gods are exalted above pleasure and pain and Aristotle's description of God as the "first cause" or "unmoved mover."

As a result, these Christian thinkers could not accept the idea of God's participation in Jesus' suffering and death, since they could not conceive of God suffering in any way, from any cause. These theologians recognized a continuity between Jesus and God in regard to the power of resurrection, but a discontinuity in regard to the humiliation of suffering and death. The power displayed in Jesus' life was "the power of God"; it could even be said that the love displayed in Jesus' life was "the love of God." But the suffering in Jesus' life must never be thought of as "the suffering of God." God had *willed* the cross:

he had *willed* to save man through Jesus' suffering, but he had not participated in that suffering.

As for the Old Testament passages which spoke of fiery passions in God, it was taken for granted that these were mere figures of speech. To accept them at face value would lead to too low a view of God, thinking of him in terms too much like those of human beings. To think of literal sorrow or pain in the heart of God, it was felt, would be inconsistent with his omnipotence and immutability. Suffering in God would make him subject to frustration and imperfection.

Until recently, the doctrine that God cannot suffer was simply assumed in most Christian theology. It is found in the writings of Tertullian, Hippolytus, Augustine, Cyril of Alexandria, Anselm, Thomas Aquinas, John Calvin, James Arminius, Stephen Charnock and John Wesley.[3] That the majority of Reformation and post-Reformation theologians upheld the doctrine is evidenced by the explicit reference to it in the Thirty-Nine Articles of Religion and the Westminster Confession of Faith.

In contrast to this long-standing tradition, the twentieth century has seen a reaction—indeed, something of a revolt—against the doctrine of impassibility. Literally hundreds of respected Bible scholars, theologians and Christian philosophers have argued vigorously in favor of divine passibility. The following statements are indicative of this movement:

The doctrine of the impassibility of God, taken in its widest sense, is the greatest heresy that ever smirched

Christianity; it is not only false, it is the antipodes of truth. It is the negation of Christ's message. By this door has entered false thought and false conception of every kind. That God can and does suffer in relation to His sinful creatures—this is a cardinal doctrine of Christianity.[4]

Now there can be little or no doubt that the noblest quality in human nature is man's ability to love; and the New Testament unequivocally affirms that "God is love." But love always involves the risk—indeed, in a fallen world, almost the certainty—of suffering. So this inevitably raises the question of the alleged "impassibility" of God. It is manifestly inadequate to suggest that it was only the human nature of Jesus which suffered in the garden, on the cross, and when he wept over Jerusalem, for it was the whole person who underwent these experiences. Nor can we confine the concept of divine suffering to the human life of the incarnate Lord; . . . for the yearning love of God for his wayward people is clearly revealed in the book of Hosea and in many other parts of the Old Testament. . . .

God himself suffers when we sin, and he suffered more than we can begin to understand when, in Christ, he "reconciled the world to himself."[5]

Who is right, the earlier theologians or these more recent ones? Does God suffer? Are the Old Testament references to suffering in God really only figures of speech? Was the cross of Jesus Christ meant to reflect the reality of a cross in the heart of God? These questions will be the subject of the next two chapters.

3

The Cross in the Old Testament

As we read about God in the Old Testament, a wonder, a compassion, a secret glory begins to emerge. In books such as Isaiah or Hosea we may feel we are on the verge of penetrating through the Shekinah cloud to something unspeakably holy enthroned at the center of the universe, something which gives the universe its reality and defines its significance. The reason is that the prophets of Israel had caught a glimpse of the Creator:

When a prophet of the LORD is among you,
 I reveal myself to him. . . . (Num 12:6)
Surely the Sovereign LORD does nothing

without revealing his plan
to his servants the prophets. (Amos 3:7)
What did God reveal about himself to the prophets?
Might part of that revelation concern his suffering?

In order to answer this question we must first consider two Old Testament themes—the wrath of God and the love of God.

The Divine Tension
It is impossible to read the Old Testament and not to notice that God's attitude toward his people is sometimes one of wrath. We may be repelled by the idea of divine wrath, but we should not react by treating it allegorically. God is depicted as genuinely angered by our sin, even fiercely angered. The severity of this anger cannot be diluted, for it finds intense expression in nearly every book:

See, the Name of the LORD comes from afar,
  with burning anger and dense clouds of smoke;
his lips are full of wrath,
  and his tongue is a consuming fire. (Is 30:27)

Who can withstand his indignation?
  Who can endure his fierce anger?
His wrath is poured out like fire;
  the rocks are shattered before him. (Nahum 1:6)

God created us to love one another, to treat each other with respect, justice and kindness; but he also gave us the gift of free will. As a result we are free to choose instead the way of exploitation, injustice and corruption. God's wrath reflects his absolute, inflexible opposition to these paths:

Hear this, you who trample the needy
*   and do away with poor of the land. . . .*

The LORD has sworn by the Pride of Jacob:
*   "I will never forget any thing they have done.*

"Will not the land tremble for this
*   and all who live in it mourn?" (Amos 8:4, 7-8)*

I will punish the world for its evil,
*   the wicked for their sins.*
I will put an end to the arrogance of the haughty
*   and will humble the pride of the ruthless. (Is 13:11)*

In addition God made us to love and have fellowship with him. We sinned not only against our brother, but against our Creator. The tragedy about which the Old Testament writers are most burdened is that of our rebellion against the Most High. The fellowship of God and man has been severed, and iniquity is rampant throughout the earth:

"Be appalled at this, O heavens,
*   and shudder with great horror," declares the LORD.*
"My people have committed two sins:
They have forsaken me,
*   the spring of living water,*
and have dug their own cisterns,

broken cisterns that cannot hold water.''
(*Jer 2:12-13*)

When we recognize that these verses apply today,
that all of us have forsaken our Creator and his righteous ways to pursue paths of selfishness, which is
the essence of sin, we find ourselves filled with horror
and shame. Furthermore, if we are attuned to God,
we are awed that the omnipotent God, who justly
could have destroyed the world, rather continues
to sustain it. Why does God allow a creation, which
is in rebellion against him, to continue to exist at all?

The words of Moses, addressed to his rebellious
generation, give the answer: "For the LORD your God
is a compassionate God; He will not fail you nor destroy you. . . . Because He loved your fathers, therefore He chose their descendants after them" (Deut 4:
31, 37 NASB). The mysterious fact of God's love for us
is everywhere proclaimed by the Old Testament
writers. He loves us as a father loves his son:

"I have loved you with an everlasting love;
    I have drawn you with loving-kindness. . . .
Is not Ephraim my dear son,
    the child in whom I delight?
Though I often speak against him,
    I still remember him.
Therefore my heart yearns for him;
    I have great compassion for him,'' declares the
    LORD. (*Jer 31:3, 20*)

God's love is not a faint, passing impression, but a
deep, overwhelming one which is firmly rooted in
his eternal character. His love is deeper and more

perfect than that of a mother for her child:

Can a mother forget the baby at her breast
    and have no compassion on the child she has borne?
Though she may forget,
    I will not forget you! (Is 49:15)

In the Old Testament these themes—the wrath of God and the love of God—are found side by side. Abraham Heschel writes, "It is as if there were a dramatic tension in God."[1] How can we reconcile the tenderness of divine love with the vehemence of divine anger? Heschel suggests that between the word of wrath and the word of compassion, between "consuming fire" and "everlasting love," there is a "hidden bond." Let us probe these themes of love and wrath more deeply to see if we can uncover this hidden bond.

First, we should recognize the dominance of God's love:

"In a surge of anger
    I hid my face from you for a moment,
but with everlasting kindness
    I will have compassion on you,"
    says the LORD your Redeemer. (Is 54:8)

God is described as having not only love for us, but *everlasting* love. Love is his dominant attitude, not wrath. The New Testament even goes so far as to proclaim that God *is* love. Never do we find the phrase "everlasting wrath" and only once the phrase "wrathful God." It is always the "compassionate God" who may for a time be angered.[2]

Love is a constant, contingent on nothing. It is always freely bestowed. Wrath is a temporary state occasioned only by our sin. Wrath signifies a genuine state of anger, but it stems from love. It is an expression of concern, never a desire to retaliate.

Second, we find that God's love motivates him to accomplish a "new work" in his relationship with us in our estrangement. Because a change has taken place in us, because we have turned our backs on God, God's love must manifest itself differently from what it did prior to the Fall. It is not that his love diminishes, it is that there must be a change in the *working out* of the love which itself remains constant. But how should we understand this working out of God's love?

Does God's love become indifferent? Does he simply begin to ignore a facet of our behavior. But "indifferent love" is a contradiction in terms. Love implies deep concern about every aspect of the object of that love, and it rules out the possibility of indifference. If God were indifferent to sin, the word *love* could never be used to describe his attitude toward us.

We might suppose, on the other hand, that God's love has been defeated. If so, then perhaps God's reaction to sin is one of lowering his ideals for his creation and admitting defeat. We might then think that God still loves us, but accepts a world of disharmony. The prophets, however, never suggest a passive work of acceptance, but a mighty new work of reconciliation and restoration.

The Hidden Bond
God's purposes cannot be frustrated. Despite our sin

God has continued to seek us out, first calling out a people for himself and then, after delivering them from bondage in Egypt, establishing a covenant with them on Sinai. Still his people wandered from him, and yet he promised a new covenant that would accomplish all that he had planned from the first and that would include men and women from every nation. " 'This is the covenant I will make with the house of Israel after that time,' declares the LORD. . . . 'I will forgive their wickedness and will remember their sin no more' " (Jer 31:33-34). God's love moves him to accomplish a new work of *forgiveness*, to turn people back to himself and eventually to restore harmony in the world through the total destruction of sin. God's love is a forgiving, transforming love. But what, we may ask, does God's forgiveness cost him? For us, forgiveness means the joy of reconciliation and the hope of a new heaven and earth. But what has the work of forgiveness meant for God?

The prophets saw that God's forgiveness meant suffering for him. Suffering is the hidden bond between love and wrath. In a phrase, God's attitude toward us as revealed in the Old Testament is "*suffering* love":

> *In the moment in which man sinned against God, God gathered into His own heart of love the issue of that sin, and it is . . . by the mystery of the passion of God, that He is able to keep His face turned in love toward wandering men, and welcome them as they turn back to Him. Had there been no passion in His heart, no love, no suffering of Deity, no man could ever have returned to him.*[3]

The cost of our forgiveness is that suffering in the heart of God which alone made it possible. Without suffering there is no forgiveness. You may say that the wrongdoer ought to bear the brunt of his own evil deed; but the whole meaning of forgiveness is that he does not and the other does.[4]

I think it can safely be said that when we speak of the cross in the Old Testament most people think of certain prophetic passages. The cross is thought to be a New Testament event which is only foreshadowed in the Old. A passage such as the story of Moses lifting up the serpent in the desert (Num 21:9; Jn 3:14) comes to mind.

The cross, however, is not just a matter of prophecy in the Old Testament. When we speak of the sacrifice of the cross, we speak not just of a New Testament event but of an Old Testament event as well. As G. Campbell Morgan has said, "That which we see in the Cross did not begin at the point of the material Cross."[5] Sin has been a crucifixion of God from the foundation of the world.

The apparent conflict of love and wrath in the Old Testament reveals suffering at the heart of God:

When Israel was a child, I loved him,
    and out of Egypt I called my son.
But the more I called Israel,
    the further they went from me.
They sacrificed to the Baals
    and they burned incense to images.
It was I who taught Ephraim to walk,

taking them by the arms;
but they did not realize
    it was I who healed them. (Hos 11:1-3)

How can I give you up, Ephraim?
    How can I hand you over, Israel? . . .
My heart is changed within me;
    all my compassion is aroused.
I will not carry out my fierce anger,
    nor devastate Ephraim again.
For I am God, and not man—
    the Holy One among you.
    I will not come in wrath. (Hos 11:8-9)

Return, O Israel, to the LORD your God,
    Your sins have been your downfall!
Take words with you
    and return to the LORD.
Say to him:
    "Forgive all our sins
and receive us graciously,
    that we may offer the fruit of our lips. (Hos 14:1-2)

How moving these insights into God's character are!
God is tender and compassionate like a father teaching his son to walk. And he suffers when his children turn their backs on him.

In Hosea 11:8 when God says, "My heart is changed within me; all my compassion is aroused," the Hebrew word translated "changed" literally means "turned over."[6] In the context here it describes upheaval, turmoil. The word translated "aroused" literally means "contracted" and implies that God's compassion is deeply affected, even to the point of being in spasm. God is saying, "My heart is moved to its depths! I am in turmoil."

We cannot write off these expressions of God's deep emotion and many others like them elsewhere in the Old Testament as mere attributions of human emotion to God. Since we are made in the image of God and he describes himself as suffering, we have little, if any, reason not to take these expressions at face value. If God is indeed like us, as we are like him, what reason, apart from some prior philosophical commitment, have we to think that God does not suffer? So long as we do not imagine that God is tossed to and fro by emotional upheavals or that he alters his purposes in response to such yearnings, we gain more from learning that God is able to understand and enter into our struggle than from holding that he is remote and unaffected by it.

Even as early a record as Genesis records God's pathos:

> The LORD saw how great man's wickedness on the earth had become.... The LORD was grieved... and his heart was filled with pain. (Gen 6:5-6)

God is called "the rock" in the Old Testament, but Moses knew the name did not imply hardness of heart:

> The whole Israelite community set out from the Desert of Sin, traveling from place to place as the LORD commanded. They camped at Rephidim, but there was no

water for the people to drink. So they quarreled with Moses and said, "Give us water to drink."

Moses replied, "Why do you quarrel with me? Why do you put the LORD to the test?"

But the people were thirsty for water there, and they grumbled against Moses. They said, "Why did you bring us up out of Egypt to make us and our children and livestock die of thirst?"

Then Moses cried out to the LORD, "What am I to do with these people? They are almost ready to stone me."

The LORD answered Moses, "Walk on ahead of the people. Take with you some of the elders of Israel and take in your hand the staff with which you struck the Nile, and go. I will stand there before you by the rock at Horeb. Strike the rock, and water will come out of it for the people to drink." So Moses did this in the sight of the elders of Israel. (Ex 17:1-6)

God had delivered the people from bondage. They had witnessed miracle after miracle wrought by God's grace. Now, a few months later, the Israelites face some hardships, and they decide they can no longer trust God. He would never turn his back on them, but they are ready to turn their backs on him.

The staff, the symbol of divine judgment, should rightly fall on the Israelites, but the picture here is of man ascending to the throne of judgment. The staff is taken by man and is allowed to fall on God by God's own command. The rock which Moses strikes is the heart of God, and the water which flows is the forgiving love for which man so desperately thirsts. The name *rock* signifies God's immutable will to redeem, whatever the cost in suffering to himself.

Theocentric Understanding

The discussion so far may have come as somewhat of a surprise. "God suffers for sin like this in the Old Testament? I thought this was true only of Christ in the New Testament." As Abraham Heschel points out, this central Old Testament category for God has often been overlooked even by theologians:

> The bricks we collect in order to construct the biblical image of God are, as a rule, conceptual notions such as goodness, justice, wisdom, unity. In terms of frequency of usage in biblical language, they are surpassed by statements referring to God's pathos, which, however, for a variety of reasons, has never been accorded proper recognition in the history of biblical theology.[7]

No attempt will be made here to identify all the reasons God's suffering has often been overlooked, for it would take us beyond the scope of this book. But I would like to briefly identify two reasons.

One is the failure to read the Old Testament from God's perspective, or theocentrically. This was illustrated in the above discussion of forgiveness. As readers of the Old Testament we tend to concentrate so much on the implications of forgiveness for us (reading *ego*centrically) that we fail to consider its implications for God. And by failing to consider the texts from God's point of view, we miss the revelation of God's suffering.

This is true as well for the theme of the prostitute. Ezekiel writes:

> *And your fame spread among the nations on account of your beauty, because the splendor I had given you made your beauty perfect, declares the Sovereign LORD.*
>
> *But you trusted in your beauty and used your fame to become a prostitute. You lavished your favors on anyone who passed by and your beauty became his.*
> (Ezek 16:14-15)

When we hear God speak of his people this way, many of us react by examining our own lives to see any ways in which we might be living as a prostitute in God's eyes. We turn inward and become introspective because God sounds angry. We read the passage egocentrically, taking it as a revelation about our sinful selves. This is not entirely wrong. In part, we should read the passage in this manner.

But we should also attempt to cultivate a God-centered consciousness that would take in the full meaning of the passage. Failure to understand the passage theocentrically is to miss half the meaning. There is an appeal in these words to examine not only our own inner lives, but the inner life of God. We must ask what God is saying about *himself* by describing the object of his love as a prostitute. There is more in his voice than anger.

Consider a related Old Testament motif—that of the rebellious child. The following passage opens the book of Isaiah:

> *Hear, O heavens! Listen, O earth!*
> *For the LORD has spoken:*
> *"I reared children and brought them up,*
> *but they have rebelled against me.*

The ox knows his master,
   the donkey his owner's manger,
but Israel does not know,
   my people do not understand." ...
They have forsaken the LORD;
   they have spurned the Holy One of Israel
   and turned their backs on him. ...
   Why do you persist in rebellion? (Is 1:2-5)

At first glance it may appear that this text teaches only
two truths: that man has sinned and that God is
angry. But if we listen more carefully to the tone of
these words, we find that God is revealing something
of the depths of his heart in this passage. He is la-
menting. There is an element of tragedy in God's
voice. It is always *"my* people ... *my* children have
rebelled against *me."*

The Old Testament metaphors of the prostitute
and the rebellious child point not only to our sin but
to God's pain. Behind his anger God is saying, "I ache
that my beloved has become a prostitute; I am pained
that my children have rebelled."

Divine Strength in Weakness

Another reason for the lack of emphasis on the suffering of God is the fear of ascribing to God an attribute
which would be inconsistent with his omnipotence
and immutability.[8] We noted this fear in the last chapter. Objectors hold that suffering in God implies
weakness and frustration. One writer states that a
suffering God becomes "the most miserable object of
our pity," for he must be at the mercy of his creation.[9]

Many of the objections to passibility are dispelled when we keep in mind that God has *chosen* to forgive, *chosen* to suffer. Faced with the scandal of human sin, he could have destroyed the world entirely. The story of the flood is set before us as a symbol of this possibility. But instead, in his great love, he chose to forgive through suffering:

God is passible in the sense that he really suffers for the sins of men; they are, quite simply, agony to him.
... [But] *he suffers because by the act of creation he has so placed himself that if man sinned it meant suffering for God. No man could make God suffer without the divine consent.* [10]

The God of suffering does not passively endure pain, but actively chooses to embrace it.

God's strength is made manifest in the weakness of suffering. His sacrifice reveals the strength of his love. God's suffering is not inconsistent with his omnipotence; it is an expression of it. In 1 Corinthians 1:18-31, Paul identifies the suffering Christ as "the power of God." This "weakness" of God is the most powerful force in the universe (1 Cor 1:25). The love which causes God to submit to suffering is the love of a strong God.

Contrary to the dominant strain in theology, we have found that suffering is *not* foreign to God's experience even as recorded in the Old Testament. In the next chapter, we will see that this also is the teaching of the New Testament. The New Testament writers found a link, not a gap, between the suffering of the Messiah and the nature of God.

4
Jesus, the Heart of God

The most disturbing and the most provocative teaching in all the Bible is that Jesus Christ, the son of a simple carpenter from the town of Nazareth, was in reality God in human flesh. It was this truth which so motivated the early church.

The early church thrived on the conviction that in Jesus Christ God had visited and redeemed the world. The gap between God and man was bridged. The Incarnation marked the turning of a glorious new page in human history. New Testament Christians believed that God himself had come near to them, living among them incognito, concealing himself in human form. The next step was to recognize in this concealing of his deity, a revealing of God's nature.

The Image of God

Long ago the Hebrew prophet Isaiah asked a question which echoed the religious speculations of all mankind: "To whom, then, will you compare God? What image will you compare him to?" (Is 40:18).

This question was answered in various ways according to men's presumptions about the Deity. For example, some thought of God as all-powerful, so they constructed the image of Hercules—a tall, muscular figure who possessed superhuman strength. This is what they figured God was like. Others thought of God as ruler and judge, so they formed the image of Jupiter—a venerable figure grasping thunderbolts. To them this was a better representation.

For the Hebrew, however, the question was rhetorical. The answer was that there is no one to whom the Lord God can be compared, no image which adequately reflects his being (Ex 8:10; 9:14; Deut 33:26; Ps 86:8; Is 44:7). Any image, whether animate or inanimate, which someone might label a representation of God would in fact be a misrepresentation according to the Jews, for they knew their God to be beyond comparison.

In light of the Incarnation, however, this situation suddenly changed. No human being or marble statue could represent God, but God-in-the-flesh could represent God! Jesus Christ could be known as the image

of God because he was the *uncreated* image of God.
The question, "To whom will you compare God?"
can be answered, "To Jesus Christ," because Jesus
was God.

Three times in the New Testament Jesus is called
the image of God: in 2 Corinthians ("Christ, who is
the image of God"—4:4), in Colossians ("He is the
image of the invisible God"—1:15) and in Hebrews
("his Son... the express image of his person"—1:2-3
KJV). Paul uses the Greek word *eikōn* in 2 Corinthians and Colossians; the writer of Hebrews uses the
word *charactēr*. Let us look at the meaning of each of
these words.

1. eikōn. This Greek word, from which we de-
rive the word icon, was used for that which was a
precise copy or accurate representation. Often the
word was used to contrast with that which was a
vague and imperfect reproduction.

William Barclay points out two particular uses of
the word which are significant.[1] The form *eikōnion*
corresponds to our modern "photograph." And so in
an ancient letter we read of a soldier writing home to
his father, "I send you a little portrait *(eikōnion)* of myself done by Euctemon." The word *eikōn* has an even
more suggestive use. It was used for the official, accurate description of a person, written up and at-
tached to business documents. This paper was the
means by which a person could be identified, for it
detailed his personal characteristics.

Paul is saying to those who want to know what
God is like that Jesus is the perfect portrait of God.

In Jesus we see God unveiled; he is the manifestation of God's character. In Jesus, that which was previously unknown and undiscerned about God's nature becomes knowable and discernable; in Jesus the invisible God becomes visible.

And this must be understood in light of the centrality of the cross. The entire New Testament was written round the cross. For Paul especially, the gospel was the word of the cross: "we preach Christ crucified" (1 Cor 1:23); "for I resolved to know nothing while I was with you except Jesus Christ and him crucified" (1 Cor 2:2). The entire body of Paul's writings sprang from the cross: "The cross . . . was *the* act of God. It was absolutely central. All that Paul was, and all that Paul hoped for, centered on the action of God in the cross."[2]

So when Paul calls Jesus the image of God, he is saying, "When you see Jesus *on the cross* you see the perfect portrait of God. In Christ *crucified* you see God unveiled." Paul saw no inconsistency between the sufferings of the Messiah and the nature of God. For Paul, the crucifixion of Jesus meant the crucifixion of God and was the means by which God's suffering love was revealed.

2. *charaktēr.* This is the word from which we get our word *character.* In the Greek world it referred to the sharply defined impression made in clay, wax or metal by a seal or diestamp. If anything, the relationship between Jesus and God is made even more explicit by this word than by *eikōn.*

Nothing can be more like the original mold or seal

than the image pressed out on the clay or wax, the one carrying the very form of features of the other. The O.T. saints did not perfectly "express" God, nor can angels, for they are but finite creatures; but Christ, being Himself God, could and did. All that God is in His nature and character is expressed and manifested, absolutely and perfectly, by the Incarnate Son.... Though we had never seen the seal we might, from beholding the impress of it (that which is exactly like it), form a true and accurate idea of the seal itself.[3]

Various English translations of Hebrews 1:3 highlight nuances of the meaning: "the express image of his person" (KJV); "the exact representation of his being" (NIV); "the very stamp of his nature" (RSV).

The word translated "person," "being" or "nature" is *hypostasis*, which literally means "that which stands underneath." In the context here it refers to the inward nature of God which underlies his various actions or relations with others. So in Jesus we may not see the full extent of God's omnipotence, we may not see God in his omnipresence, we may not see God in his majestic heavenly glory, but we do see God in his character. Jesus is the embodiment of God's nature.

This phrase, "the express image of his person," is coupled with the complementary expression "the Son is the radiance of God's glory," which further conveys the meaning. The imagery here is of beams of light issuing from the sun, penetrating the darkness of the universe. The glory of God "is not any external halo that surrounds the divine nature; it is

the divine nature itself in its majesty and as manifested to the world."⁴ In Exodus 19 we find that God's
glory is his goodness. What the writer of Hebrews
is saying is that Jesus is the shining forth of God's
goodness among men, the "outraying"⁵ of his redemptive love for the world.

He Who Has Seen Me Has Seen the Father

Jesus repeatedly taught the disciples to see in his life,
not just the works of a great human being, but the
very life and works of God (Jn 5:19, 8:28-29, 10:37-38).
In John 14 he declares to Philip, "Don't you know
me, Philip, even after I have been among you such a
long time? Anyone who has seen me has seen the
Father."

The apostle John's reflections on this truth is suc-
cinctly and profoundly stated in the prologue to his
Gospel:

> *In the beginning was the Word, and the Word was with*
> *God, and the Word was God. . . . And the Word be-*
> *came flesh and dwelt among us, full of grace and truth;*
> *we have beheld his glory, glory as of the only Son from*
> *the Father. . . . No one has ever seen God; the only*
> *Son, who is in the bosom of the Father, he has made*
> *him known. (Jn 1:1, 14, 18 RSV)*

The image of Jesus which John treasured in his heart
was the image of God. John wanted everyone to share
in this wonderful knowledge, and by using the title
"Word" (or *Logos* in Greek) John captured not only a
Jewish audience but also a Greek audience. Heraclitus introduced the idea of the Logos as a technical

term into Greek philosophy as early as 560 B.C. Heraclitus observed the world around him to be in a con-
tinual state of change. He gave the illustration that
it is impossible to step into the same river twice.[6]
The second time you enter you do not really step into
the same river because the original water has flowed
on. To Heraclitus the entire world was like that.

On the other hand, Heraclitus recognized a prin-
ciple of order in the universe. Life was not total chaos.
There was a certain order and predictability to things.
Certain actions always resulted in the same reaction.
The sun would rise and set in a regular fashion; like-
wise, the seasons came in their appointed order.
What produced this order in the midst of the flux?

Heraclitus said it was the Logos, the mind of God.
The Logos was the rational principle which brought
about order in the midst of chaos, the controlling
mind which pervaded all of reality.

With this background we can understand what a
shock it must have been for Greeks to read verse 14
of John's prologue: "And the Word became flesh and
dwelt among us." The rational principle became a
living, breathing human being? Here was something
never before said by any Greek philosopher. St.
Augustine tells us that in his pre-Christian days he
had studied all the philosophers and had found all
that he desired—except this, that the Word became
flesh. To John's readers this verse must have been
startling and incredible.

Having caught the attention of his readers, John
took them a step further in verse 18. He led them to

see that he used the term "Word of God" more in line
with its Hebraic meaning than its Greek meaning.
The Greeks might speak of the Logos, but they did not
think of it as a personal God. For them it was chiefly
a principle or force.

To the Jews, on the other hand, the Word referred
to the self-expression of the living God who created
and loved the world. The Word constituted the creative extension of God's nature and character. In other
words, the Word meant God acting and revealing
himself in his wisdom and love.

Had he followed the Greek line of thought John
might have described the Word as an emanation of
the rational mind, but instead he says the Word
comes from the *bosom* or *heart* of the living God. That
makes the concept intimately personal.

Here is the keynote of John's Gospel: Jesus Christ
is the Word of God, not a vague emission from an
impersonal force, but the living expression of a living
Person—the Lord God. And so he is the Revealer of
his Father, the Revealer of his nature and of his af-
fections.

Our words are the means by which we reveal our
thoughts and feelings, but often our words are superficial, governed by whim rather than deep, inner conviction. God's Word, however, flows directly from his
innermost being. His Word is the perfect expression
of his thoughts and feelings. John is saying, "No one
has ever seen God in his transcendent glory and
heavenly majesty, but if you want to know what God
is *like*, what his attitude toward the world is, how he

reacts to sin, look at Jesus. Jesus has revealed his character. He is God unveiled. Jesus is the heart of God."

And what do we see when we look at Jesus? The answer is found in verse 14 in the word *grace*. This word, a favorite word of the New Testament writers, refers to the "extravagant goodness" of God displayed in the suffering love of the cross. The essence of grace is that God is for us, even when we are against him: "But God demonstrates his own love for us in this: While we were still sinners, Christ died for us" (Rom 5:8). Jesus brought that which was veiled into glorious visibility. He displayed God's suffering love to the whole world.

The Continuity of the Old and New Testaments

Many people have come to view the Testaments as though they were in tension or even contradictory, almost as if they were portraying two different Gods. They tend to view the God of the Old Testament as stern and avenging, and the God of the New Testament as forgiving and embracing. But the Bible knows no such dualism of God's nature.

I hope that this book will serve to counter this misunderstanding. The division of Old and New Testaments does not signify a God of wrath giving way to a God of love, but a God of suffering love in progressive revelation.

Think of Richard Strauss's *Also Sprach Zarathustra*, the music used in the film *2001*. The music begins with a low, rumbling pedal point which leads to a

trumpet call. This call then ushers in the great re-
sounding climax of the full orchestra. The last cymbal
crash of this climax is heard and the orchestra seems
to cut off, into silence. But when the reverberation
passes, the pedal point, which had undergirded the
entire development, is still heard.

The unfolding message of the Bible is like that. In
the trumpet call we hear the voice of John the Baptist
crying in the wilderness, and in the climax, the revelation of Jesus Christ. But throughout, underneath the
high notes, sounding out of the depths, is heard the
suffering love of God.

The music of the Old Testament is like those initial
moments before the trumpet call in Strauss's piece. As
we read the Old Testament we do not hear the whole
orchestra, but if we listen carefully we detect the pre-
ludial throbbing of the pedal point. The high notes
are not heard because the major revelation was yet
to come and the Old Testament writers did not know
God's *plan* fully. That is, they did not fully understand
the *means* of revelation, through the Incarnation and
Jesus' death on the cross. But they did know God's
heart and so had some understanding of the *content*
of that revelation.

All of this is to say that the Bible knows no dualism
of personality or attitude in God. He who has seen
Jesus has seen the God of the Old Testament. The
Word has always been with God and has always been
God. What changed is that in the New Testament the
Word became flesh.

In Old Testament times a few prophets perceived

God's suffering, but as for the world at large, "men did not know it, and could not understand it; and therefore God came into human form and human life, to the actuality of human suffering, on the green hill and upon the rugged Cross, working out into visibility all the underlying, eternal truth of the passion of His love, that men seeing it, might understand it, and put their trust in Him."[7]

When we recognize the crucified Christ as the image of God, we discover the eternal character of our Creator, the continuity of the Old and New Testaments, and the foundation on which the world was created.

This truth, which Greek-influenced theology missed, is the very truth which helps us in our own struggle with suffering.

5

God
Suffers
for Us

Once we have seen the vision of the crucified
God, we begin to see the light which penetrates the
darkness of human suffering. Each of the passages
we looked at in the last chapter has in its immediate
context the imagery of light shining forth in darkness.
We saw this already in Hebrews 1:3. Let us look at
three other passages:

> The god of this age has blinded the minds of unbe-
> lievers, so that they cannot see the light of the gospel
> of the glory of Christ, who is the image of God. . . .
> For God, who said, "Let light shine out of darkness,"

*made his light shine in our hearts to give us the light of
the knowledge of the glory of God in the face of Christ.
(2 Cor 4:4, 6)*

*Then Jesus cried out, "When a man believes in me, he
does not believe in me only, but in the one who sent
me. When he looks at me, he sees the one who sent me.
I have come into the world as a light, so that no one
who believes in me should stay in darkness." (Jn 12:
44-46)*

*In the beginning was the Word, and the Word was with
God, and the Word was God. . . . In him was life, and
the life was the light of men. The light shines in the
darkness, and the darkness has not overcome it. (Jn
1:1, 4-5 RSV)*

In the world's darkness, in our own darkness, Jesus
Christ, the image of God, is the shining light which
penetrates the darkness, for in him we see the revelation of God's love.

This is not an external luminosity, not a mere theological concept, but a life-changing inward illumina-
tion, for Jesus shines into our hearts the conviction
that, whatever the evidence to the contrary, at the
center of reality is not a cynical power making a mock-
ery of humankind, but a power of love reaching out
to save and heal. As Christ's arms were spread wide
on the cross, so are God's arms spread wide to the
world, nailed in devotion to its redemption.

For Paul, the light of this gospel was dazzling and

overwhelming in its splendor. On the road to Damascus Paul had seen a vision of God's redeeming love, a love which had descended deeper than sin, suffering, and even death. This Jesus was now exalted above the heavens, filling all things. This experience was not just something to write theological epistles about, but something he treasured in his heart, something he carried with him everywhere—in hardship, distress, persecution and imprisonment. The light of Jesus as the image of God enabled Paul to rejoice in hope in the midst of the most severe affliction.

He whose creative Word called light to shine forth from darkness and chaos when time began will now shine forth in our troubled hearts also "to give us the light of the knowledge of the glory of God in the face of Christ." We may have felt nothing but hopelessness in our anguish, but seeing the unveiling of God in Christ, "a better hope is introduced, by which we draw near to God" (Heb 7:19). This hope is "an anchor for the soul, firm and secure. It enters the inner sanctuary behind the curtain" (Heb 6:19). The darkness can never overpower this hope. As at the heart of a flame there is a tiny space, cool and untroubled by the outward flame, so this hope reigns in our hearts amid the fiery trials of life, producing inner victory amid outward defeat.

We may have raged at God in our pain, but we now draw near to him, for we have seen the light of his love. We understand that God is for us, not against us.

Distressed and hungry, they will roam through the land; when they are famished, they will become en-

*raged and, looking upward, will curse their king and
their God. Then they will look toward the earth and
see only distress and darkness and fearful gloom, and
they will be thrust into utter darkness. Nevertheless,
there will be no more gloom for those who were in distress. . . .*

    *The people walking in darkness
      have seen a great light;
    on those living in the land of the shadow of death
      a light has dawned. (Is 8:21–9:2)*

The Cross Divested of Its Liberating Power

I have found that some people who have heard of
Christ, and some who have even become Christians,
have never seen the light of Christ as the image of
the suffering God. For this reason they never know
the hope and comfort which comes in experiencing
the full depth of God's love. Patty, a friend of mine,
has struggled with this.

During her teen-age years Patty attended a Christian church, following her parents' wishes. Unfortunately, church was a very negative experience for
her. The services produced in her an oppressing sense
of sin and guilt, especially when anyone spoke about
the cross. It seemed to Patty that her parents and
most of the people in the church operated primarily
from this sense of sin and guilt. The only positive
feeling Patty had was the sheer ecstasy she experienced when church was over.

Tragically, the preaching in that church left Patty
right there. Because the cross was not explained with

sensitivity and insight, it became depressing news rather than good news. The cross became the symbol of the oppression in that church she grew to hate.

When I met Patty she was in her thirties. She had not attended church in fifteen years, and she recalled her teen-age experience with a great deal of loathing. Yet Patty was searching. She had experienced much suffering as a result of a divorce and was generally disillusioned with life. She wanted to know if I went to church. I told her I did and that it was not out of a sense of duty, but out of a desire to experience the joy of Christ with other believers.

"Joy?" she shouted in disbelief.

I went on then to tell her what I understood about the Incarnation and the cross. I told her that all of us are sinners deserving death, but that on the cross God died in our stead—that he freely and willingly became our substitute, himself bearing what we deserved, because of his great love for us and his intense desire that we should be reconciled to him.

Patty stopped me. She was shocked. "Did you say *God* died for us on the cross?"

I said yes, that Jesus was God in human flesh. This did not register with her, so I explained it again. I then explained it a third time. Finally she said to me thoughtfully, "I've never heard that before."

What a revolution it was in Patty's thinking to think that God himself suffered for her on the cross! My prayers for Patty's conversion have not yet been answered, but as I have watched the change which has taken place in her, I have often thought of these words from J. B. Phillips:

> Now, if the lonely figure hanging on the Cross so long
> ago were merely a great and good man, martyred for
> his beliefs, then that is regrettable, but hardly of any
> significance to us today. But if it was God who was
> murdered, if it was God who willingly allowed the
> forces of evil to close in upon him and kill him, then
> we are in the presence of something which, though it
> happened in time, is of eternal significance. We are
> looking upon something utterly foreign . . . to any
> other religion. We are seeing God allowing himself not
> only to be personally involved in the folly, sin, and
> downright evil of the human situation, but accepting
> death at the hands of his own creatures.
>
> This is . . . unknown to the majority of people. I
> believe we must use every skill of communication,
> every device of writer, artist, poet, and dramatist to
> break the insulation of ignorance and let men see who
> died upon the cross. We are without doubt in the pres-
> ence of an uncalculable mystery. It is so far beyond
> the ordinary man's ideas of God, sin, forgiveness and
> reconciliation that the mind is carried out of its depth
> and the heart is overwhelmed by the dreadful signifi-
> cance of the event. Once people begin to realize that
> the man on the cross is no demigod, no puppet-god-
> ling, no fragmented piece of godhead, but God himself,
> there is bound to be an explosion in their thinking.[1]

We who are Christians need to heed these words. We
need to let people see who it was that died on the
cross. If we fail to convey that God himself was in
Christ, Christ ends up being thought of not as the

image of God, not as the heart of God, but as the
victim of God, as some sort of third party—a little
more than human, but a little less than God—upon
whom God poured out his vindictive wrath. The end
result is that we set before a non-Christian such as
Patty a distorted view of God's character, and we inspire oppression and fear rather than hope and faith.
We divest the cross of its liberating power.

Randy's story illustrates a similar situation. God's
Spirit worked in Randy's life, convicting him of sin
and the need of forgiveness, but he did not respond
when his Christian friends witnessed to him about
the cross. After much frustration, his friends decided
that the answer was for Randy to hear some dynamic
evangelists. So, over a period of months, they took
him to hear various speakers. Many were indeed very
dynamic, yet Randy still did not respond.

One Sunday morning while watching television,
Randy accidentally turned to a religious program on
which an evangelist was preaching. The message was
much the same as what he had heard before, but this
time something different happened. As the evangelist spoke about Jesus on the cross, tears came to his
eyes. What he *said* was similar to what Randy had
heard before, but through his tears a deeper truth
was conveyed—the truth Randy had been aching to
discover.

In that moment the tears of the evangelist became
the living symbol of the tears of God. Randy saw the
face of God in the face of that evangelist. He realized
that it was God himself who hung on the cross and

who wept for him. He finally saw the light of Christ as the image of the suffering God. Randy became a Christian soon after that, experiencing to the fullest the liberating power of God's forgiveness, the joy of knowing God and the hope of being transformed into his likeness.

Care in Witness

The tragedy for those of us who are Christians is that Patty and Randy realized that God himself suffered for them not *because of* what believers had said to them, but *in spite of* what they had said. When Randy was asked what had been lacking in the explanations of the cross he had heard, he said simply this: "No one ever clearly explained that God was the one who hung on the cross for me."

What had his friends said? That Jesus was the Son of God and that he had been "sent by God" to bear sin. This kind of language is fine, as long as we are sure our non-Christian listener understands the perfect unity of Father and Son. If he does not, such language may confuse him.

Since the realization that God suffered on the cross can be the single most liberating discovery and the one leading to faith, it is vital that Christians use terminology in witnessing which will cultivate understanding of this truth and not camouflage it. Let us consider two designations for Jesus which may confuse.

1. The Son of God. This title is, of course, a valid title. It is repeatedly found in the New Testament.

The problem today is that so few people, either Christian or non-Christian, have a clear enough understanding of the Trinity to know that the Son of God is *truly* God, not some sort of subordinate or intermediate being. This is so harmful because it fosters a conception of God as distant to the event of the cross and as stern in his attitude toward people. We must always keep in mind that the phrase "Son of God" when applied to Jesus means God in the flesh.

   2. *The Second Person of the Trinity.*   Theology attempts to define the being of God by setting forth three propositions, all of which are simultaneously affirmed: (1) There is one God; (2) This God exists in three persons: Father, Son and Holy Spirit; (3) These three each possess all the fullness of deity. It admittedly seems to be a sheer contradiction to speak of *one* God in *three* persons. The difficulty has to do with the meaning of the word *person*. What theologians mean by this word and what we mean by it in everyday language are quite different things. To us, it means a separate, self-conscious individual. In theological language, it does not mean this.

   I did a one-question survey on the campus of a Christian college in which I asked students if the trinitarian phrase "three persons" referred to three individuals. A large percentage answered yes. They believed Jesus was an individual entirely separate from God the Father. This is very unfortunate, first of all, because it is wrong.

   There are three Persons, yet so as not to form separate and distinct individuals. They are three modes or forms

> *in which the divine essence exists. "Person" is, how-*
> *ever, an imperfect expression of the truth inasmuch as*
> *the term denotes to us a separate rational and moral*
> *individual. But in the being of God, there are not three*
> *individuals, but only three personal self-distinctions*
> *within the one divine essence.*[2]

Second, the concept of three individuals is unfortunate because it results in a misunderstanding of God's
nature.

In his best-selling autobiography, talk-show host
Phil Donahue lists various reasons for his disillusion-
ment with Christianity. One of the things he says is
this: "How could an all-knowing, all-loving God
allow His Son to be murdered on a cross in order to
redeem my sins? If God the Father is so 'all-loving,'
why didn't *He* come down and go to Calvary?"[3] He
says this because of a misunderstanding of the Trinity, and such misunderstanding is often caused by
Christians. The same misconception is illustrated
by the story a pastor once told about a little girl with
whom he was talking about being a Christian. When
he mentioned the importance of loving God, the girl
answered, "But I don't love God. I love Jesus, but I'm
afraid of God."

It cannot be emphasized enough that orthodox
Christianity affirms as its cardinal principle that in
Jesus of Nazareth, God himself has come near to us to
redeem, *not* a second member of a triad of individuals
to which the Father also happens to belong. Our message is that God has made a personal visit. We must
always present this with clarity and certainty.[4]

Perhaps the best definition of the Trinity is that given by Donald M. Baillie. He says that the doctrine of the Trinity is not a mysterious mathematical statement about three-in-one. What it really asserts, he says, is that it is God's nature, first of all, to *create* finite beings whom he could love (Father); second, to *redeem* them and *reveal* himself to them, even to the point of Incarnation (Son); and third, to *sanctify* them by doing in them what they could not do themselves (Spirit).[5] When we become Christians, we do not enter into three relationships. We enter into a single relationship with the one God, who is known to us *as* Father, who was present *in* Christ, and who is made real to us *by* the Spirit.

God Was in Christ

"God was in Christ reconciling the world to himself" (2 Cor 5:19 RSV mg): this, rather than complicated explanations and analogies of three-in-one and one-in-three, should be our watchword in evangelism. Statements like "the Son of God was sent to be God's provision for sin," or "the second person of the Trinity became the sacrifice for sin," often confuse non-Christians, who do not have the theological background to understand their meaning.

Using the metaphor of the theater, we can say that in the drama of redemption there are three roles; *but the three roles are played by two actors, not three.* The role of judge is played by God, the role of the accused is played by man, and the role of the substitute or Savior *is played by God,* not by some third actor.

> When we try to understand the New Testament doc-
> trine of substitution we must bear in mind the close
> unity between God the Judge and Christ the Savior.
> In the process of salvation, God is not transferring
> penalty from one man (guilty) to another man (inno-
> cent). He is bearing it Himself. The absolute oneness
> between the Father and Son in the work of atone-
> ment must not for a moment be lost sight of. When
> Christ substitutes for sinful man in His death, that
> is God Himself bearing the consequences of our sin,
> God saving man at cost to Himself, not at cost to some-
> one else.[6]

In Old Testament times, atonement was understood as
taking place externally to God, in the sacrifice of animals. God was pictured as *observing* and *accepting* the
sacrifice. There are some now who see in Christ the
ultimate external sacrifice, which, like the animals, is
observed and accepted by God. But the real meaning
of atonement as revealed in Christ is that it takes place
internally. Atonement takes place within the very
being of God. Christ is the fulfillment of the Old Testament system, but in such a way that the Old Testament system "is completely transformed into the idea
of an atonement in which *God alone bears the cost.*"[7]

When the great preacher Henry Ward Beecher first
made this discovery, he said with sublime simplicity,
"I felt I had found a God." So too when our non-
Christian friends realize that God was in Christ, suffering for them on the cross, they will feel they have
found a God. We must never tire of repeating it: God
was in Christ, himself bearing the consequences of

sin, himself redeeming us from its grip.

Some Christians feel they must stress the dreadfulness of sin and the terrors of hell in their witnessing to scare people into faith. I do not believe God would have us do this. A. W. Tozer defines faith this way: "Faith is the gaze of a soul upon a saving God."[8] This means that our primary duty is to lift up Jesus; in other words, to help the non-Christian see God on the cross. The Holy Spirit will do the work of convicting him of sin (Jn 16:8).

The cross is like a piece of glass erected before us. In one sense it is a window through which we see the merciful heart of God; in another sense it is a mirror in which we see the reflection of our own sinful hearts. We as Christ's witnesses are to present the cross as a window. The Holy Spirit quickens a person's vision to see it also as a mirror. Our job is simply to lift up Jesus, to proclaim him as the image of the suffering God.

The Shape of the Shadow of Suffering

While bringing faith to the non-Christian, the discovery of God on the cross brings hope and comfort to all of us in our distress over the world's suffering, for we see God dealing with the root cause of the world's problems. We see him grappling with the disease behind the world's symptoms.

Imagine for a moment looking at the earth from a point in space. The suffering of the world appears as a dark shadow engulfing the planet. Perhaps a wave of fear shoots through us as we feel the icy chill of that portion of the shadow which has touched our own lives.

The shadow of affliction can indeed be frightening. But when we see a shadow we usually look for the substance, the reality, behind the shadow. A shadow cannot exist in and of itself; it cannot exist in isolation. It is not a self-produced reality and so is not an ultimate thing. The shadow testifies to the existence of a light, and also to the existence of an obstruction to the rays of the light.

Picture now that as we turn our eyes from the earth we see the sun and an enormous mass directly between the two. The sun represents God, and its rays his everlasting love toward man. The obstruction is our sin. We cause the shadow, not God.

God intended for us to live in paradise. The thorns and thistles, symbolic of all pain and suffering, grew into our reality only after Adam and Eve sinned (Gen 3:18). But God has done a wondrous thing. He has begun to re-create our broken reality. He has taken the dark, ugly mass of sin and has shaped it into a cross for himself. It is now preeminently the cross which casts its shadow over human history. We determined the fact of the shadow; God determined its shape.

Why did we not recognize the shape of the cross before, when looking directly at the shadow? Then it appeared distorted and fragmented. The reason is that we lose touch with the fact that there is a light at all if we become overwhelmed or preoccupied with the shadow. We then lose sight of the shadow's uniform shape.

When the shadow of suffering falls over our lives, overwhelming us and causing us to lose all perspective, the Comforter comes to us to remind us that there is a light, to reveal the reshaped substance which casts the shadow and thereby to disclose the actual shape of the shadow. As we come to see this, we no longer live in the shadow, but in the reality. And the reality is the crucified Christ. Human pain is the shadow; divine pain, the reality.

6
God
Suffers
with Us

Our pursuit of God led us to consider the revelation of Jesus Christ. Through a survey of both the Old and New Testaments, we discovered the link between the suffering of the Messiah and the nature of God. In the suffering and death of Christ, we perceived the sacred unveiling of the suffering God. In the outwardly visible event of the crucifixion, the hidden inner life of God was revealed; the material cross revealed the eternal cross. In seeing this vision of the suffering God, we have seen how human sin affects God.

We can now see that our original question of how human suffering affects God is answered by the same vision. The divine pathos is the answer the Scripture gives to both questions. Human sin pierces God's heart; human pain grieves him. In the life of Christ we see God not only bearing sin, but also bearing the human suffering which results from sin. He suffers *for* man to save; he suffers *with* man to strengthen and comfort. This is the full meaning of divine suffering love. This love is almost beyond our comprehension. Through Christ, God is revealed as the devoted Creator who embraces the broken reality of his fallen creation, as the Great Burden-bearer, who in his own heart bears the onslaughts of *all* destructiveness.

The Man of Sorrows

In my own experience the discovery of God's participation in human suffering was actually more influential in my religious life than the discovery of his suffering for sin. It resulted in my becoming a Christian. I was much like Ivan Karamazov—I believed in the existence of God, but I could not accept the world of suffering I saw around me.

For instance, I would watch the successive tragedies on the evening news and be genuinely troubled. It affected me; it mattered to me. People would say, "There's nothing you can do about it, so just forget it." The problem was that I knew God should be able to do something about it, so I was unable to forget.

As I understood the Christian message, God was concerned about our need for redemption from sin and was personally involved in bringing it about. But he seemed distant and unmoved by our suffering.

This distressed me terribly; in fact, it angered me greatly. I could never worship a God who was indifferent to human affliction. I hated this God.

I identified not only with Ivan Karamazov, but also with Doctor Colin in Graham Greene's *A Burnt-Out Case*. In the novel, Colin, a confessed atheist, works among severely afflicted people at a leper colony run by priests and nuns. At the end of the book Colin stands with the Father Superior, observing the appalling suffering and grotesque mutilations of the many patients. He turns to the Father and suggests that his God must be pained as he looks at the suffering of the world. The Father then says, "When you were a boy, they can't have taught you theology very well. God cannot feel disappointment or pain." Doctor Colin replies, "Perhaps that's why I don't care to believe in him."

That's exactly how I felt. When Christians witnessed to me I would find myself asking, "But how does God feel about all the tragic suffering that goes on in the world? What goes on in his mind? Don't you watch the news? Where is God when an innocent child is mangled in an accident or born deformed?" I actually never heard a direct theological reference to the impassibility of God as in the response of Greene's Father Superior, but what I did hear amounted to much the same thing—impassive, abrupt answers like "I'm sure it is not in his perfect will." Or "Certainly it does not please him to see people suffer." Most people got defensive and seemed threatened by my questions.

Then one day I spoke with a gentleman who seemed far more understanding. As I watched him, I could see in his eyes that he too had been troubled by the problem of pain or else had experienced great suffering himself. To my surprise, he was not afraid to admit that the suffering of the world made faith in God difficult; yet, and this was what really struck me, he was not threatened in his own faith. When I asked him about this confidence, he did not attempt long explanations but rather suggested that I read an Old Testament passage—Isaiah 53. Again I was impressed. He didn't nervously bombard me with dozens of memorized verses, as many others had. He so deeply believed what this one passage said that he felt it was sufficient. I went straight home and looked it up in my Bible.

As I read the chapter I was convinced that I was being exposed to something infinitely sacred. Somehow in these words there was truth, the truth I had been searching for:

> He was despised and rejected by men,
>   a man of sorrows, and familiar with suffering. . . .
> Surely he took up our infirmities
>   and carried our sorrows. (Is 53:3-4)

I was deeply moved. Tears came to my eyes, but I was also confused. What did this mean? Who was this man, and why was he suffering? The meaning of the words seemed just beyond my grasp.

In my mind's eye I envisioned the man. I pictured him slowly walking across a rugged terrain. He was hunched over, carrying this enormous burden on his shoulders. He was in great pain, almost crushed by the load, but he kept on because he possessed some incredible, superhuman strength. I sensed that his heart was about to break from the knowledge of the contents of this encumbrance, but still he kept on. It was not physical strength. It was an inner strength which was definitely not of this world. I felt it was the strength of pure, unselfish love.

This vision was the most beautiful thing I had ever seen. I felt like the merchant in the parable who was willing to sell everything he had when he came upon the pearl of great price. But who was this strange man, and what was the huge weight he was carrying?

For the next week I did little else but think about Isaiah 53. I went through the motions of my daily work and activities, but inside I kept pondering the mystery of the man of sorrows. The vision of him was continually in my mind. That Saturday I went to the library in hopes that I might find some answers. I decided to take out a life of Christ entitled *God So Loved the World*. It was through this book that I discovered the identity of the man of sorrows.

The next morning I opened to chapter one. I still experience a sense of wonder when I read those first sentences. They turned my life upside down:

This is the story of an almost unbelievable humbling, nothing less than the story of the life that God lived when he came down from heaven and lived upon earth as a man. In a particular human body, born of a Mother belonging to a certain race of people, nearly two thousand years ago in the country of Palestine, God lived and died for us men and for our salvation.[1]

Finally the light began to dawn. I had always been

drawn to Jesus Christ because he so identified with all who suffered. In the tenderness of his compassion, he would hurt with those who were hurting. Now I finally understood this in light of the Incarnation. This adorable beauty of Jesus Christ which had always drawn me was the beauty of God. The man of sorrows was Jesus Christ, and Jesus Christ was none other than God in the flesh. The vision of the man of sorrows carrying his burden now merged with the New Testament image of Christ carrying his own cross to be crucified, and I knew that the cross represented not only human sin, but also human suffering: "Surely he took up our infirmities and carried our sorrows." Verses in the New Testament I had not understood before came alive to me. For instance, Christ's words in the Garden of Gethsemane: "My heart is ready to break with grief" (Mk 14:34 NEB). Part of the reason he said this was that he was carrying the weight of the world's suffering.

Tears of joy began to flow. I knew the answer to my question, "How does God feel about the world's suffering?" I knew that human suffering breaks God's heart.

God hates to see his children suffer. He hates it so much that he bears the brunt himself. Every loss, every cancer, every agony is part of the burden God carries. No one suffers alone. He suffers with us: "When you pass through the waters, I will be with you.... Since you are precious and honored in my sight, and because I love you, I will give men in exchange for you.... Do not be afraid, for I am with you" (Is 43:2-5).

Have you ever wondered if God cares about your illness, your loneliness, your erring child, your broken home? Here is the answer: Fix your eyes on Jesus; his heart is ready to break with grief. He who has seen Jesus has seen the Father.

Another passage of Scripture which has come to mean much to me in the same way is found in John 11. This scene occurs just before Christ raises Lazarus from the dead:

When Mary reached the place where Jesus was and saw him, she fell at his feet and said, "Lord, if you had been here, my brother would not have died."

When Jesus saw her weeping, ... he was deeply moved in spirit and troubled. "Where have you laid him?" he asked.

"Come and see, Lord," they replied.

Jesus wept. (Jn 11:32-35)

Kent Hughes comments on the meaning of this text:

The word for "was deeply moved" comes from an ancient Greek word that describes a horse snorting. When taken in this text's context, it implies that our Lord let out an involuntary gasp. The wind just went out of him. E. V. Riev translates the thought, "He gave way to such distress of spirit as made His body tremble." The point is that our Lord was so caught up in the sister's emotion that he involuntarily gasped. He felt their sorrow with everything he had. Notice the verse ends by saying "he was troubled." That enlarges the thought. That means he voluntarily took their sorrow to himself. Mary and Martha's sorrows were taken to his heart.

> *Finally we come to that great word, "Jesus wept."*
> *The word means tears ran down Jesus' face. Here we*
> *have a great God who loves us . . . who allows us to*
> *go through ultimate extremity, and then comes and*
> *enters into our sorrow. He enters the sorrow . . . in*
> *such a way that he gasps, his whole body shudders*
> *and he begins to weep. That is the perspective that*
> *Christ wants us to have.*[2]

The great unseen reality behind the visible world of
suffering is the suffering God who feels the agony of
every loss, the stab of every pain. As hymnwriter
F. W. Faber puts it:

> *There is no place where earth's sorrows*
> *Are more felt than up in heaven.*

I had thought God to be a spectator; I now knew him
to be the main participant in the arena of suffering.
What a revolution in our thinking when we view God
no longer as cold or indifferent but as intimately and
poignantly involved with us!

God's Fellow-Suffering

Korean Christians have been sustained by this belief that God suffers with us. Dr. Chung-Hyun Ro of
Yonsei University in Seoul writes:

> *For the Korean Church in particular, the last century*
> *has been one of continual conflict and suffering. . . .*
> *Through all this struggling, it has been our conviction*
> *that God never stood aloof, that He has never turned*
> *His back, that always He was suffering with us, as*
> *Christ demonstrated. It is this very fact which has been*
> *—and still is—our hope.*[3]

The importance of this belief is reflected in the theme chosen for the Seoul Theological Consultation of 1979: "The Hope: God's Suffering in Man's Struggle." For a Korean involved in the painful struggle for peace, justice and human dignity, the discovery of God's participation is life-changing. It brings strength, hope and comfort. The same can be true for us in our struggles.

The English author and preacher Leslie Weatherhead made this discovery of God's fellow-suffering. In one of his books he describes a dream in which he is standing in heaven next to an angel, looking down on suffering humanity. As he listens, he hears the cries of people in pain all over the world, and he becomes very angry. He wonders how God can dwell in transcendent serenity while all humanity is in such turmoil.

> *In my dream the angel turned to me a face which I cannot describe. There was pain in it such as I had never seen in a face before. Yet there was joy too outshining it. There were tears in his eyes. Yet through the tears a triumph shone. And he spoke to me. When he spoke, I knew that there was not a pang of pain on earth that was not shared in heaven. More, I knew that what men suffered on earth was only a faint reflection of the anguish God and his holy angels endured on man's behalf in heaven. Somehow it came to me that through all its pain, which he more than shared, God with man was working out the world's redemption.*[4]

In the *Chronicles of Narnia*, C. S. Lewis takes his character Digory through a painful experience, one in which he makes the discovery of God's fellow-suffering. Digory approaches Aslan the Lion, creator of

Narnia, to ask for some magical fruit to make his ail-
ing mother well. He fears that the matter might be
considered insignificant to the Lion, but he gets up
the courage at least to ask.

When the Lion doesn't even answer, Digory is
stunned. It appears that Aslan doesn't care at all about
Digory's anguish or his mother's illness.

At first Digory can't say anything, but then as he
recalls all of the great hopes he had had and how they
now were dying away, tears fill his eyes and he approaches the Lion a second time. To his surprise,
Digory finds that he and his mother hadn't been
the only ones suffering:

> Up till then he had been looking at the Lion's great
> front feet and the huge claws on them; now, in his
> despair, he looked up at its face. What he saw sur-
> prised him as much as anything in his whole life. For
> the tawny face was bent down near his and (wonder of
> wonders) great shining tears stood in the Lion's eyes.
> They were such big bright tears compared with Dig-
> ory's own that for a moment he felt as if the Lion must
> really be sorrier about his mother than he was himself.[5]

After this experience Digory never again doubted the
love of Aslan: "whenever he remembered the shining
tears in Aslan's eyes he became sure."[6] My experience
has been much the same. The vision of the suffering
God has reoriented my entire perspective and issued
in a new level of trust. I believe I can trust in the goodness of God despite the existence of human, unmerited suffering; not because someone told me God is
good, but because I have seen for myself the biblical

vision of *divine*, unmerited suffering. In the assurance of God's suffering love I can proclaim with Habakkuk:

> Though the fig tree does not bud
>   and there are no grapes on the vines,
> though the olive crop fails
>   and the fields produce no food,
> though there are no sheep in the pen
>   and no cattle in the stalls,
> yet I will rejoice in the LORD,
>   I will be joyful in God my Savior. (Hab 3:17-18)

I do not have answers to all my questions, and I still find myself confused and angry at things God allows to happen. I continue to express these feelings to God honestly. But I now find it possible to *trust* him. I no longer picture affliction as something borne by man and observed by a distant God, but as something God and man, side by side, bear together, with God bearing the worst of it. This recognition of God's participation sometimes causes me to shrink back and cover my mouth in horror. He loves us so much, at such cost to himself, it is almost too much. Whenever the vision of the man of sorrows comes into my mind, I can barely stand to look into those eyes which tell the agony of God. I am sure it was this very feeling which Isaiah meant to convey when he described those who see the vision:

> Kings will shut their mouths because of him.
> For what they were not told, they will see,
>   and what they have not heard, they will understand. (Is 52:15)

Immanuel—God with Us

In answer to the sufferer's cry "Where are you, God?" God teaches a name, the name *Immanuel*. When it comes to the problem of pain, the Lord is much more than a God who "watches over us." He is Immanuel, "God with us." He more than sympathizes; he becomes involved:

> The LORD himself goes before you and will be with you; he will never leave you nor forsake you. Do not be afraid; do not be discouraged. (Deut 31:8)

It is vital that we recognize the full implication of the name *Immanuel*. God identifies with human suffering in all ages. He did not just *once* suffer, *once* identify with us, in the first century. It is true that during Jesus' earthly life God lived among us in a unique way. Nevertheless, God has always been, and always will be, Immanuel.

This timelessness of divine immanence seems to have been in the mind of Matthew when he wrote his account of the "good news." He begins by informing us that the story of Jesus which he is about to tell is the story of "God with us" (Mt 1:23). He then concludes his gospel by returning to this idea, but *not in the past tense* as we might expect. He doesn't say, "Truly we have seen and believed that in Jesus God was with us." Rather he quotes the words of Christ: "And surely I will be with you always, to the very end of the age" (Mt 28:20). Here is God's good news to sufferers: "Fear not, I am with you *now*. I am always Immanuel."

Where is God when it hurts? He dwells with us

from the beginning to end, as the Silent Sufferer, and throughout he bears all the violent attacks of destructiveness in his own heart. God is closer to our suffering and its agony than we are ourselves.

Meaningless suffering intensifies when it is borne alone. Sufferers then need not merely sympathy, but genuine empathy. They need "someone who *understands*" to be there, to stand with them in their hour of trial. In the coldness and alienation of a hospital bed, it means so much to be affirmed by the warm embrace of a friend who understands what the affliction is like, someone who has experienced the same pain and the same fear.

Some of us may be fortunate enough to have someone who is able to empathize in this way. Others of us may not. But we all can have the assurance that God empathizes. He *really understands*. He knows. He always empathizes, for he feels our sorrow as his own.

Certain passages in the Old Testament bring out this beautiful truth. For example, in the book of Exodus the Lord says: "I have seen the affliction of my people who are in Egypt. . . . I know their sufferings" (Ex 3:7 RSV). The Hebrew word *yada* (translated "know") means far more than mental apprehension. It denotes inner engagement and feeling, personal involvement, a reception into the soul.[7] When God says, "I know their sufferings," he is saying, "I am *affected* by their sufferings. I *feel* their sufferings." The idea is stated most explicitly in Isaiah: "In all of their distress he too was distressed" (Is 63:9). These texts demonstrate God's personal involvement in human suffering. They show us that God was Immanuel even before the Incarnation.

As I have been saying, he also is Immanuel following the resurrection. A short time after the ascension, Saul is stopped on the road to Damascus by the voice of Christ, "Saul, Saul, why do you persecute me?" (Acts 9:4). Notice that he doesn't say, "Why do you persecute my church?" but, "Why do you persecute *me*?" Though he is no longer physically present, he still identifies, he is still involved, for he indwells his people (see Mt 25:31-46). This identification is so complete that to persecute the church is to persecute him.

If the people of God suffer, God suffers. If a child is injured, God is injured. He is Immanuel. He is closer to our suffering and its agony than we are ourselves.

Peace I Leave with You

Some of us are undoubtedly bothered by the fact that the *cause* of unmerited suffering is left unanswered by God. The question "Why?" plagues us. Why are there natural disasters such as tornadoes and earthquakes which kill innocent people? Why does God allow birth defects? Why doesn't he stop this suffering?

Part of the answer to these questions is that God *is* going to stop all suffering at some point in the future. Any discussion of suffering is incomplete without this perspective on its temporary nature. Suffering will not always be a part of human existence. In

heaven there will be no more pain or death, and one
day on the earth itself suffering will cease:

> On this mountain the LORD Almighty will prepare
>   a feast of rich food for all peoples,
> a banquet of aged wine—
>   the best of meats and the finest of wines.
> On this mountain he will destroy
>   the shroud that enfolds all peoples,
> the sheet that covers all nations;
>   he will swallow up death forever.
> The Sovereign LORD will wipe away the tears
>   from all faces;
> he will remove the disgrace of his people
> from all the earth.
>
> The LORD has spoken. (Is 25:6-8)

The resurrection of Jesus Christ was a sign of this
coming resurrection of all humanity.

Whether in heaven or on a restored earth, I know
that one day I will live in perfect harmony, free from
evil and suffering. My faith in this great future hope
helps sustain me in the present.

But still many of our whys are left unanswered, and
the fact is that God doesn't give answers to all our
questions. Throughout the Bible we are steered away
from the question of cause to the question of response, away from "Why did this terrible thing happen?" to "How shall I deal with this terrible thing?"
Jesus did not come giving answers to all our questions
about the origin of evil powers, but to defeat those
powers and to help us deal with them prior to their
total annihilation at the end of the age. He came not

giving answers, but giving himself.

Through Christ, God put to death the worst of agonies—our feeling of abandonment. And in giving himself, he has given us peace—not a peace which ends our wars with pain and evil, but one which gives us the strength and comfort needed to live victoriously in a world in which pain and evil are yet to be put away: "I have told you these things, so that in me you may have peace. In this world you will have trouble. But take heart! I have overcome the world" (Jn 16:33). In parts of the church some teach that a Christian should never suffer. Those who teach this may be sincere (they are probably reacting desperately to the sometimes unbearable extent of suffering in our world), but it simply is not what the Bible teaches.

According to the world, of course, peace means the absence of war, the absence of conflict. So it is somewhat natural to assume that Christ's promise of peace implies freedom from affliction. But Jesus said, "Peace I leave with you; my peace I give you. I do not give to you as the world gives" (Jn 14:27). God gives us a peace which is not of this world, nor is it understood by the world. Paul speaks of "the peace of God, which transcends all understanding" (Phil 4:7).

According to the Bible the peace which God gives is not a freedom from the storms of life, but a mysterious strength and comfort amid the storms; not the removal of pain, but the bestowal of a precious gift. The gift is God himself, the Comforter, the one who "stands alongside us."

Feelings and Fellowship

Though in an overriding and abiding sense I believe
God has put to death our feeling of abandonment,
I feel I must qualify the statement. I do not mean to
paint a rosy picture of suffering. Pain hurts! And
often pain is very lonely. It is not as though Christians
walk tranquilly hand in hand with God through all
hardship. During my own times of greatest suffering,
feelings of betrayal and abandonment have often
gripped me rather than joy and peace. Sometimes I
have felt totally alone, as though God were against
me and not for me. Then I have felt not trust in him
but doubt, not love for him but anger and even hate.

The awareness of God's presence and of his being
on my side has come only in retrospect, long after the
dark depression has passed. After the ordeal I have
been able to say that I know God was with me and for
me, but any momentary sense of these truths during
the ordeal resulted more from the active, hard work of
believing by faith, *despite feelings to the contrary*,
rather than through passive acceptance. In times like
this, God's peace isn't like a blanket which a father
drapes over his child, but like a blanket at the end of
the bed which the child must pull up. The father
provides the blanket, but the child has to put forth
much of the effort. Receiving God's peace may not be
automatic; it may require the work of faith.

When we find our faith to be weak and we feel
abandoned by God in our pain, we must cling to him
all the more, for he experienced the same struggle
during his days on earth. He knows what it is like.

Though Jesus is God, he also is fully human, and in that humanity he experienced the same feelings of abandonment. On the cross he cried, "My God, my God, why have you forsaken me?" God identifies with us in suffering even to this point. In fact, he goes beyond this.

Jesus in his deity experienced a dreadfulness of abandonment and aloneness the hour he uttered these words which is infinitely beyond our comprehension. As Martin Luther once said, "God forsaken of God! Who can understand that?"[8] We may *feel* abandoned, but we are never actually alone. He passed through the outer darkness, suspended between heaven and hell, totally alone.

How do we respond to a God who has done so much to redeem us? In the New Testament concept of "sharing in the sufferings of the cross" we find part of the answer. This higher dimension of the human-divine fellowship in suffering will be discussed in the chapter which follows.

7

The Sufferer's Imitation of God

As I read the New Testament I am stunned by the barrage of adversities encountered by the early church. The hardships endured by just one individual, the apostle Paul, far surpass what seems reasonable for any ten people to endure. Taken together, Paul's sufferings exceed those of Job. He writes:

> *Rather, as servants of God we commend ourselves in every way: in great endurance; in troubles, hardships and distresses; in beatings, imprisonments and riots; in hard work, sleepless nights and hunger. (2 Cor 6:4-5)*

> *I have worked much harder, been in prison more fre-*
> *quently, been flogged more severely, and been exposed*
> *to death again and again. Five times I received from*
> *the Jews the forty lashes minus one. Three times I was*
> *beaten with rods, once I was stoned, three times I was*
> *shipwrecked, I spent a night and a day in the open sea,*
> *I have been constantly on the move. I have been in*
> *danger. . . . I have labored and toiled and have often*
> *gone without sleep; I have known hunger and thirst*
> *and have often gone without food; I have been cold and*
> *naked. (2 Cor 11:23-27)*

We may think that because he lived at the time of
Christ and wrote much of the New Testament, Paul
had some sort of supernatural halo about him, in-
sulating him and enabling him to transcend all feelings of despair. This simply is not true. Paul did not
glide through his afflictions on a cloud of bliss. In
words similar to the lamentations of Job, Paul writes:
"We do not want you to be uninformed, brothers,
about the hardships we suffered in the province of
Asia. We were under great pressure, far beyond our
ability to endure, so that we despaired even of life.
Indeed, in our hearts we felt the sentence of death"
(2 Cor 1:8-9). These words reveal an experience of
intense anxiety.

How did Paul understand these adversities and
feelings? In chapter four we saw how the New Testament church interpreted the sufferings of Jesus. We
now ask how the New Testament church interpreted
its own sufferings.

Participating in the Sufferings of the Cross

In one of his books F. J. McConnell writes:

> *The Christian comes after a while to realize that the greatest part of the pain which he suffers is not his, but God's. God is not sharing his pain as truly as he is sharing God's. Then he sees that in a measure he is privileged to share the suffering of the cross.*[1]

This is exactly what happened for Paul and the New Testament church. Since Christ suffered in his work to usher in the kingdom of God, and since they were now "in Christ," they could expect to suffer in his footsteps: "Therefore, since Christ suffered in his body, arm yourselves also with the same attitude. . . . Dear friends, do not be surprised at the painful trial you are suffering, as though something strange were happening to you. But rejoice that you participate in the sufferings of Christ" (1 Pet 4:1, 12-13). This included the agony of feeling abandoned. Jesus had felt abandoned in Gethsemane and on Calvary; his followers might therefore experience the same thing: "You will indeed drink from my cup. . . ." (Mt 20:23).

I fear that many of us have not fully grasped the cost of being a disciple of Christ. We live in a country where there is little danger of being persecuted for professing Christ. It is even fashionable to be "born again." And when sufferings other than persecution come upon us, we nearly relinquish the faith. Even mere inconvenience causes us to falter. What a contrast to the New Testament church! They found their very identity in the crucified Christ.

Helmut Thielicke was once asked what in his

opinion was the most important issue facing American Christians. He replied, "They have an inadequate view of suffering." His words ring true. Many of us are willing to witness about the cross, and this is good. But we are also called on to follow the example of the cross. To be a Christian is to witness to the suffering of God and to enter that suffering. How often we try to ignore the second aspect! When Paul says, "Join with me in suffering for the gospel," we answer, "No, thank you." But can we do this and legitimately call ourselves Christians?

A missionary to Kenya, having detailed the fiery ordeals of Christian converts there, including the threat of mutilation and death by terrorists, wrote, "I am constantly humbled by their patience and lack of bitterness which springs from an acceptance of the Cross in their lives."[2] These words condemn most of us. I feel that condemnation myself.

Perhaps we have to reconsider the cost of discipleship, what it means to "be imitators of God" (Eph 5:1). Christ was exalted in sacrifice. What does it now mean for him to be exalted in us? Over 170 times Paul uses the phrase "in Christ." Have we really accepted the implications of our being united with him?

It may be more popular, and certainly it is less threatening, to think in terms of a gold cross or a smooth cross, but an old rugged cross is the true symbol of Christianity. It has been said that any Christian who has not had the feeling he must flee the crucified Christ has not understood him in a sufficiently radical way. Since the cross, the problem of pain is no longer something to debate, it is "a staggering election."[3]

Perhaps we have to rediscover suffering. Some of our contemporaries seem to be telling us this:

Our officially optimistic society believes in the idols of action and success. Through their compulsive inhumanity, they lead many persons into apathy and despair. The churches in this society often function as nothing more than religious establishments, caretakers for the idols and laws of this society. If this society is to turn itself toward humanity, the churches must become Christian. They must destroy the idols of action and apathy, of success and anxiety; proclaim the human, the suffering, the crucified God; and learn to live in his situation. They must discover the meaning of suffering and sorrow, and spread abroad the spirit of compassion, sympathy, and love.[4]

Dietrich Bonhoeffer proclaimed a similar message:

Christians range themselves with God in his suffering; that is what distinquishes them from the heathen. . . . It is not some religious act which makes a Christian what he is, but participation in the suffering of God in the life of the world.[5]

It is a need of the hour that American Christians understand their obligation to participate in the messianic sufferings of God in Christ. This need becomes all the more urgent as suffering in our world increases.

It is all too common to regard suffering as an unfortunate interruption in the Christian life. According to the New Testament it is a *calling* in the Christian life: "we are heirs—heirs of God and co-heirs with

Christ, if indeed we share in his sufferings" (Rom 8:17); "for it has been granted to you on behalf of Christ not only to believe on him, but also to suffer for him" (Phil 1:29); "now I rejoice in what was suffered for you, and I fill up in my flesh what is still lacking in regard to Christ's afflictions" (Col 1:24); "so that no one would be unsettled by these trials. You know quite well that we were destined for them" (1 Thess 3:3); "to this you were called, because Christ suffered for you, leaving you an example, that you should follow in his steps" (1 Pet 2:21). If, in our suffering age, we fail to recognize this calling, we will retreat from the world, and we will become bitter when misfortune does touch us. Our love will grow cold and we will no longer be sons of God's light in a world of darkness.

The Gospel writers have given us an image, a picture to think of in regard to this calling. It is the picture of Simon of Cyrene: "As they led him away, they seized Simon from Cyrene, who was on his way in from the country, and put the cross on him and made him carry it behind Jesus" (Lk 23:26). As Abraham is the father of faith, Simon is the father of cross-carrying.

Now following Simon's example will mean something different for each of us: "Take up *your* cross and follow me." Each person has a different cross. And I am not saying that all troubles we face are part of God's suffering. But sometimes when we suffer, especially when the suffering follows a *choice* to sacrifice and serve others, we will have the experience of seeing ourselves in the place of Simon. We will recognize that it is actually Christ within us bearing the on-slaughts of pain, that God is not sharing our suffering as truly as we are sharing God's; and we will understand that we are creative coworkers with him in the continuing redemptive work which began at Calvary.

Sometimes we will be able to see the redemptive good our suffering generates, sometimes we will not, but from heaven's vantage point we will see and we will rejoice. At present we may see only the pain, but in the end we will see only Jesus.

We Should Not Seek Suffering

In any discussion on participating in the cross there is always the danger of extremism. For instance, there is the tendency in mystical Christianity to seek pain and hardship in hope of attaining a deeper union with the suffering God.

Although such intentions may be sincere, they are not biblical. The Bible never teaches that we should seek pain:

> Not that we should seek pain—Jesus certainly did not do so, having asked God just before his crucifixion: "Father, if it be possible, let this cup pass from me" (Matt. 26:39). Nevertheless, He went on, "not as I will, but as Thou wilt." Men do not know themselves as followers of Christ . . . until they take something of the same attitude.[6]

The Bible teaches that we should seek only Jesus, and this means we should seek love. Love is the goal of the Christian life, not suffering (1 Cor 14:1; Eph 5:1-2; 1 Tim 1:5). We are not to have a morbid obsession with suffering (see Phil 4:8).

God is not suffering. God is love. Because he is love he takes on suffering: "The nobleness of Christ's passion is that it was not a work of asceticism, a sought-after mortification, but merely the faithfulness of love."[7] This is the pattern we are to follow. If we purpose in our hearts to love, we can be sure that suffering will come our way: "Be imitators of God . . . and live a life of love, *just as Christ loved us and gave himself up for us*" (Eph 5:1-2). How did Christ love us? By loving to the point of personal sacrifice and suffering. The question is: Are we willing to love to this extent?

In a recent visit to the United States, Mother Teresa said that in her travels she has observed that love is increasing in many nations. More and more people are sensitive to the needs of others and are willing to give. But she said that one thing is still lacking—people are not willing to give until it hurts, as Jesus did.

We Should Not Accept Suffering

We should not accept suffering. What I mean by this is that our attitude toward suffering should not be one of gloomy submission or passive resignation, and, most of all, it should not be one in which we affirm suffering as being good. Good can and will come of our experience of suffering, but this does not mean we should venerate suffering itself as good.

Indeed our imitation of God should lead us to hate suffering as an enemy, not welcome it as a friend. Look at Jesus. He unequivocally declared war on all suffering, disease and death. He hated to see people suffer and healed all that were brought to him (Mt 4: 23; 8:16; 9:35; 14:14 and so on). An amazing amount of space in the Gospels is devoted to the healings of Jesus. This underscores for us that the problem of pain is a matter for action.

Because God works to fight suffering, so should we—vigorously. We should use every means at our disposal to combat suffering—prayer, medicine, social action, relief work, and so on—and our attitude should be to regard it as an enemy.

Have you ever felt anger welling up within you when you see someone in pain? This feeling is not wrong or un-Christian. It is even proper to hate our own suffering. It is right to hate loneliness, or disease, or the death of a loved one.

The image of the suffering God we see on the cross is the image of a "protesting God."[8] There we see how much God hates suffering. This is why the God of the poor and the oppressed has always been the crucified Christ.[9] They do not see in him another "poor devil" like themselves. They see an angry God who rallies to their side and who hates suffering as much as they do. It was the vision of the protesting God which strengthened Martin Luther King, Jr., in his courageous fight against human injustice and deprivation.

Have you considered the implications of the protesting God? Most of us do everything possible to combat our own suffering, but what about the suffering of others? We live in a country of affluence. Have we considered those who do not even have food or

shelter? The Bible tells us to remember those in affliction as though we ourselves were suffering (Heb
13:3). Yet how often we look the other way! We find
all sorts of reasons to avoid taking action and making
sacrifice, when inside we know that personal gain
and avoidance of the cross are the real motives.

We who are honestly committed to following
Christ must recognize him as the protesting God and
ask what sacrifices we are being called on to make in
joining his war against suffering.

The Call to be Longsuffering

What should our attitude be when we encounter personal suffering which proves to be chronic? It may
seem contradictory to speak of rediscovering and embracing suffering on the one hand, and of hating suffering and regarding it as an enemy on the other, but
I think both are part of a normal and constructive
attitude. Such ambivalent feelings coexisted in
Christ. He dreaded his suffering, he hated it, yet he
also embraced it because he knew that only *by* suffering could he destroy it (Heb 2:14).

The biblical term *longsuffering* best summarizes
this paradoxical situation:

> *To suffer is to be a victim; to be longsuffering is in a
> sense to be free. To earn the description "longsuffer-
> ing" we have to make a decision for what we do not
> want, choose to live indefinitely with what we hate.
> This is the paradox that makes longsuffering a crea-
> tive art of living.... We are talking about digging in
> daily, renewing over and over again our decision to*

accept what we desperately do not want and cannot change, making no bones about not wanting it and yet determining to live with it and rejoice in it.

Longsuffering, therefore, is the power to be a creative victim. Longsuffering is not passive. It is a tough, active, aggressive style of life. It takes power of soul to be longsuffering.[10]

To be longsuffering is to bear courageously with what we hate, knowing that a right attitude toward suffering is the alchemy which transforms it into spiritual gold. To be longsuffering is to endure something bravely, even while we reject it, knowing that our crosses are somehow part of the ongoing redemptive process and that only by this process will suffering finally be destroyed.

The model for longsuffering is God (Ex 34:6; Ps 78; Ps 86:15; 2 Pet 3:9), so our contemplation of him leads us to persevere. The writer of Hebrews tells us to keep our eyes fixed on Jesus who endured the cross. When we consider his example of longsuffering, we are encouraged to follow in his steps (Heb 12:2-3).

Why choose to be longsuffering? First, because it brings blessing to ourselves: "Blessed is the man who perseveres under trial" (Jas 1:12). It proves to us that our faith is genuine (1 Pet 1:7), and it produces character: "Consider it pure joy, my brothers, whenever you face trials of many kinds, because you know that the testing of your faith develops perseverance. Perseverance must finish its work so that you may be mature and complete, not lacking anything" (Jas 1:2-4); "we also rejoice in our sufferings, because we know that suffering produces perseverance; perseverance, character; and character, hope" (Rom 5:3-4).

Second, we choose longsuffering because it brings blessing to others. When Christians see us endure, they will be encouraged to endure themselves, and the courage displayed in our endurance will help to convince non-Christians of the authenticity of our faith. When non-Christians see us stand firm in the faith, when humanly speaking we should deny it, they may come to realize that this all-surpassing power is from God and not fabricated by ourselves (2 Cor 4:7).

In Christ, with Christ, suffering becomes a powerful means of evangelistic communication. Paul says that God put his followers "on display" in their suffering (1 Cor 4:9) so that the world might witness the operation of the supernatural in their lives. About 150 years after Paul wrote this, Tertullian said that he and most Christians were converted to Christ, not by books or logic or clever persuasion, but by observing how Christians lived, suffered and died.

In the words of Leslie Weatherhead, those who are longsuffering "achieve an enrichment and growth in personality which makes them centers of influence and light in ways which they never suspected the possibility. Few things can so inspire and re-create the human heart as the spectacle of crushing misfortune cheerfully and heroically borne, and the unconscious influence which those exert is far greater than they or others comprehend."[11] For anyone who cares about the spreading of the gospel, this is a strong motivation to be longsuffering. Our longsuffering can result in another's conversion.

Finally, we should choose to be longsuffering because it brings blessing to God. In preparing to write this book I came across a verse which I had never noticed before: "You are those who have stood by me in my trials" (Lk 22:28). Think about that. *"You ... have stood by me."* We would expect it the other way around. This is an amazing statement and its relevance extends far beyond the original hearers. Christians in every age may stand by Jesus in his trials. When we persevere in adversity we bring comfort to the suffering God. It means something to him.

Perhaps when we feel like complaining or becoming bitter, we will hear the words from Gethsemane: "Could you men not keep watch with me for one hour?" (Mt 26:40). *Our suffering is an opportunity to stand by Christ in Gethsemane.* Are we willing to stand by him who always is willing to stand by us?

The Power to be Longsuffering
The power to be longsuffering is in God himself. In 2 Timothy, Paul reveals how this power operates in our lives.

In 2 Timothy Paul speaks with unusual sensitivity and understanding about suffering in the Christian life. Affectionately he recalls Timothy's struggles and tears (1:4) and then says, "You then, my son, be strong in the grace that is in Christ Jesus" (2:1). Twice Paul encourages him to "endure hardship," and four other times he mentions endurance. Paul is saying to Timothy and to us, "Hold your head high in adversities. Hang in there. I know it's hard, but keep persevering."

But *how* can we endure? Some of us have suffered for so long. How can we go on? Where is the power to endure the unendurable?

The words of 2 Timothy 2:8 may at first fail to catch our attention as we read along. They may appear unimpressive and inconsequential. They do not seem weighty. In actuality, the key to all the power of the universe lies in this verse, waiting to unlock a vast storehouse for our use: "Remember Jesus Christ, raised from the dead" (2 Tim 2:8). Here is the answer. Here is how we find the power of God in our lives— by contemplating the resurrection of Jesus Christ.

The cross of Jesus Christ was this world's darkest hour. For a few days it appeared as though God had been defeated and all hope was destroyed. Jesus' body lay mutilated and lifeless. But the cross was matched by the resurrection. Jesus rose again from the dead. His body was restored to pulsing vitality. This was not a fanciful identification of the disciples' wishes with reality; it was an historic event to which they were "eyewitnesses"—they saw him, touched him, talked with him. And this was the supreme exhibition of the victory of good over evil. Hopelessness was transformed into hope, darkness became light, defeat became victory. In the knowledge of this, Paul says he endures everything (2 Tim 2:10).

It was not just that Paul remembered Christ's resurrection, but that he *anticipated* his own resurrection. He knew that even as Jesus was raised, so would he be raised by that same power (1 Cor 6:14).

Likewise, our hope today is not merely "I have sorrow but at least Jesus' sorrow was turned to joy," but rather "My sorrow also will be turned to joy!" Not "I have to go on suffering but at least Jesus was raised up," but "I will be raised up just like Jesus!" Endurance through contemplating Jesus' resurrection means endurance through anticipating one's own.

So whatever you are praying for today, if you have confidence before God that it is a worthy prayer, keep trusting him to answer that prayer. He is able to make all grace abound to you; he is able to give far beyond what you ask or think and he is willing to do so. Believe in the power of prayer, for you pray to the God of all power. Remember Jesus Christ raised from the dead!

But what about unanswered prayers? As the title of a recent book put it, "What about us who are not healed?" Trust on the basis of God's Word that, in God's wisdom, it is only a delay, not a denial. Even if that prayer goes unanswered throughout this life, know that it is *still* only a delay. That which you so earnestly desire will yet be yours.

Here is a hope the non-Christian world knows nothing about. Christians live in anticipation of the glory to be revealed with Christ in heaven. I am convinced that as affluence diminishes in this country and suffering, poverty and hardship become more common, those who remain joyful in confident antici-

pation of the coming glory will be the effective witnesses.

You can experience that joy in whatever situation
you find yourself today. Have you had a serious illness or accident and fear you will always be crippled?
Remember Jesus Christ, raised from the dead. You
will not always be crippled. His resurrection means
the loss which you now mourn you will ultimately
regain in heaven. You may be handicapped now,
but it's not forever. Don't torture yourself, trying to
mortify that desire to walk again, or to see again, or
to regain mental health, thinking this would please
God. God wants to restore you to wholeness. Look
forward to it. Hold on to your desire and know that
one day it will be fulfilled.

Do you fear you will never marry? Remember Jesus
Christ, raised from the dead. His resurrection means
that the desire which now goes unsatisfied will be
satisfied in heaven, and not in a less fulfilling way
but in a more fulfilling way—in the very way you
have desired and even beyond what you have desired. You might say, "But there is no marriage in
heaven." That is true, but the reason is that there
is something far better. The intimacy and fellowship
which your married friends experience is only the
shadow of a magnificent, undreamed-of heavenly
reality, and you will enter into the heavenly reality
with a unique depth of appreciation and fulfillment.
The resurrection means that those who suffer the
greatest loss at the hands of the world will enjoy the
greatest uplifting at the hands of Christ.

Blessed are you who are poor in spirit, for the kingdom of heaven is yours. Blessed are you who mourn, for you will be comforted beyond what you can imagine. Blessed are you who have been brought low, for you will be exalted. Believe it because you have seen the resurrection of Jesus Christ.

Perhaps you feel like a failure in life. You may feel like a washout as a Christian even though you honestly have turned your life over to Christ and do your very best. Again, remember his resurrection. You are not a failure. In earthly terms Jesus was the ultimate failure. He came to usher in the kingdom of God, yet he died on a cross, a nonachiever, a total loser. The resurrection assures us that our lives are of infinite value in God's eyes and have infinite purpose no matter how often we fail, no matter what the world thinks, and no matter what the world may do to us. As resurrection came for Jesus, that is, as vindication came for Jesus, so it will come for us. We are each precious and our lives here on earth are indispensable.

If you have been enduring excruciating physical pain, keep your eyes fixed on Jesus. Consider the following description of the kind of death he experienced:

For indeed a death by crucifixion seems to include all that pain and death can have of horrible and ghastly —dizziness, cramp, thirst, starvation, sleeplessness, traumatic fever, tetanus, shame, publicity of shame, long continuance of torment, horror of anticipation, mortification of untended wounds—all intensified just

*up to the point at which they can be endured at all,
but all stopping just short of the point which would
give to the sufferer the relief of unconsciousness.*

*The unnatural position made every movement pain-
ful; the lacerated veins and crushed tendons throbbed
with incessant anguish; the wounds, inflamed by ex-
posure, gradually gangrened; the arteries—especially at
the head and stomach—became swollen and oppressed
with surcharged blood; and while each variety of
misery went on gradually increasing, there was added
to them the intolerable pang of a burning and raging
thirst.*[12]

From this learn that God himself has endured un-
speakable physical agony just like you. He knows
what your pain is like. But remember the resurrection. Remember that Jesus came through to the other
side, raised in a glorious new body, forever free from
pain and suffering. In like manner, you too will be
raised up.

Many people today have experienced the pain of
divorce. This can be a living death. If you are in this
place, it probably feels like nothing, not even Jesus,
can make things right. Yet even in this situation,
rather especially in this situation, remember his
resurrection.

Jesus knows what it is like to be rejected. He came
into the world to his own, to mankind, his beloved.
He came to accept and to be accepted, to understand
and to be understood, to make things right, to love
and to triumph in that love. Yet as John writes, "He
came to that which was his own, but his own did not

receive him" (Jn 1:11). His attempt ended in bitter disappointment. He was rejected, misunderstood, ridiculed, betrayed and crucified.

Even today the great tragedy continues. Things still are not right. By all appearances, estrangement and evil will prevail to the end. As I look at the world I cannot conceive of any way that God can bring about perfect good. Crucifixion, it seems, will be the outcome of history, not resurrection—meaninglessness, not meaning.

But this is where we must wrench ourselves from the stranglehold of appearances and focus on Jesus Christ: "At present we do not see everything subject to him. But we see Jesus..." (Heb 2:8-9). Keep your thoughts fixed on him. Though he died, yet he lived. He came through to the other side. And we too will come through. God has confirmed his pledge to us through Jesus' resurrection. Things may be so dark for you right now that your very existence seems a living death, but in the midst of your hell the risen Christ makes the promise: "He who believes in me will live, even though he dies" (Jn 11:25). I don't know how this can be, I don't know how things can be made right, but Easter does not depend on my understanding.

So whatever your situation, whatever your pain, whatever your unfulfilled dreams, whatever your loss—remember Jesus Christ, raised from the dead. Never think you are trapped in the grip of the evil one, doomed to a life of misfortune and lack of fulfillment. Nothing, no power of evil or suffering, not even death, has final authority over you; only the power of the risen Christ has. All things are yours through him (Rom 8:32; 1 Cor 3:21-22). Everything, every good and perfect thing you could desire, you will inherit if you are Christ's. In a sense, all things are yours even now. By faith you participate in the inheritance. Don't think that the best things in life are passing you by or slipping away. *They are all yours as a Christian.*

The impact of this truth cannot be overestimated. Joni Eareckson, a quadriplegic and leader of an outreach ministry to the disabled, has seen it transform the lives of handicapped people throughout the world. Recently she had an opportunity to speak to a group of mentally retarded adults. Most of the people were staring out the window or up at the ceiling, nearly oblivious to her—until she began talking about the resurrection. She described how one day she would have hands that worked and feet that would walk. She spoke vibrantly, as though she had them already. Instantly there was silence and attentiveness in that room. She then said, "And one day you guys will have new minds!" Everyone stood up and cheered and applauded.[13] This is what Peter meant when he spoke of "a living hope through the resurrection of Jesus Christ" (1 Pet 1:3). In anticipation of our inheritance in Christ, we find the power to be longsuffering.

Have you felt there is no comfort? Remember Jesus Christ, crucified. His crucifixion reveals a suffering God, who cares, who is *for* you, who feels with you.

Have you felt there is no hope? Remember Jesus Christ, raised from the dead. His resurrection reveals a conquering God, who will bring you through pain, sorrow and death itself to a new life in which the problem of suffering will be solved and perfect happiness and wholeness will be realized.

Notes

Chapter 1 The Sufferer's Pursuit of God
[1]C. S. Lewis, *A Grief Observed* (New York: Bantam Books, 1976), p. 5.

[2]Fyodor Dostoyevsky, *The Brothers Karamazov* (New York: Dell, 1956), p. 173.

[3]David M. Howard, *How Come God?* (Philadelphia: A. J. Holman, 1972), p. 110.

[4]J. I. Packer, *Knowing God* (Downers Grove, Ill.: InterVarsity Press, 1973), p. 32.

Chapter 2 The Messiah and His Cross
[1]T. H. Jones, "David," *The New Bible Dictionary*, ed. J. D. Douglas (Grand Rapids: Eerdmans, 1962), p. 296.

[2]William Barclay, *Jesus As They Saw Him* (Grand Rapids: Eerdmans, 1962), pp. 88-89.

[3]See J. K. Mozley, *The Impassibility of God* (Cambridge: Cambridge Univ. Press, 1926), pp. 7-126; Marshall Randles, *The Blessed God: Impassibility* (London: Charles H. Kelly, 1900), pp. 4-15.

[4]Douglas White, *Forgiveness and Suffering* (Cambridge: Cambridge Univ. Press, 1913), p. 84.

[5]Norman Anderson, *The Mystery of the Incarnation* (Downers Grove, Ill.: InterVarsity Press, 1978), pp. 151-52.

Chapter 3 The Cross in the Old Testament
[1]Abraham J. Heschel, *The Prophets*, 2 vols. (New York: Harper Torchbooks, 1969-71), 1:46.

[2]Heschel, *The Prophets*, 2:71.

[3]G. Campbell Morgan, *The Bible and the Cross* (London: Westminster, 1930 reissue), p. 56.

[4]Douglas White, *Forgiveness and Suffering* (Cambridge: Cambridge Univ. Press, 1913), pp. 77, 81, 100.

[5]Morgan, *The Bible and the Cross*, p. 55.

[6]G. Campbell Morgan, *Hosea: The Heart and Holiness of God* (Grand Rapids: Baker, 1974 reprint), pp. 130-31.

[7]Heschel, *The Prophets*, 2:2.

[8]For a fuller discussion of the objections to passibility and suitable responses, see George A. Buttrick, *God, Pain and Evil* (Nash-

ville: Abingdon, 1966), pp. 84-97; H. Wheeler Robinson, *Suffering, Human and Divine* (London: SCM Press, 1940), pp. 159-82; S. Paul Schilling, *God and Human Anguish* (Nashville: Abingdon, 1977), pp. 235-60; T. E. Pollard, "The Impassibility of God," *Scottish Journal of Theology* 8 (1955): 353-64; Kenneth J. Woollcombe, "The Pain of God," *Scottish Journal of Theology* 20 (1967): 129-48.

[9]Marshall Randles, *The Blessed God: Impassibility* (London: Charles H. Kelly, 1900), p. 176.

[10]Bertrand R. Brasnett, *The Suffering of the Impassible God* (London: SPCK, 1928), pp. 11-12.

Chapter 4   Jesus, the Heart of God

[1]William Barclay, *The All-Sufficient Christ* (Philadelphia: Westminster, 1963), pp. 59-60.

[2]Leon Morris, *The Cross in the New Testament* (Grand Rapids: Eerdmans, 1965), p. 181.

[3]Arthur W. Pink, *An Exposition of Hebrews*, 3 vols. (Grand Rapids: Baker, 1954), 1:35.

[4]A. B. Davidson, *The Epistle to the Hebrews* (Edinburgh: T. & T. Clark, 1950), p. 41.

[5]Marvin R. Vincent, *Word Studies in the New Testament*, 4 vols. (New York: Charles Scribner's Sons, 1918), 4:382.

[6]William Barclay, *The Gospel of John*, 2 vols. (Philadelphia: Westminster,1975), 1:34.

[7]G. Campbell Morgan, *The Bible and the Cross* (London: Westminster, 1930), p. 57.

Chapter 5   God Suffers for Us

[1]J. B. Phillips, *Good News* (New York: Macmillan, 1963), pp. 173-74.

[2]R. A. Finlayson, "Trinity," *The New Bible Dictionary*, ed. J. D. Douglas (Grand Rapids: Eerdmans, 1962), p. 1300.

[3]Phil Donahue, *Donahue, My Own Story* (New York: Fawcett Crest, 1979), p. 122.

[4]In stressing the unity of God as I have, I do not mean to deny the biblically revealed reality of Father, Son and Holy Spirit. Orthodoxy has always rightly affirmed that Father, Son and Holy Spirit are coequal, coeternal distinctions within the one, indivisible divine essence. But the unity of the divine essence has often been

ignored in relation to the problem of suffering.

[5]D. M. Baillie, *God Was in Christ* (London: Faber and Faber, 1948), p. 122.

[6]Leon Morris, *The Cross in the New Testament* (Grand Rapids: Eerdmans, 1965), p. 410.

[7]D. M. Baillie, p. 175.

[8]A. W. Tozer, *The Pursuit of God* (reprinted Wheaton, Ill.: Tyndale, n.d.), p. 89.

Chapter 6   God Suffers with Us

[1]Elizabeth Goudge, *God So Loved the World* (London: Hodder and Stoughton, 1951), p. 9.

[2]From a sermon entitled "Lazarus, Come Forth!" by Kent Hughes, Pastor of College Church in Wheaton, Illinois, October 26, 1980.

[3]Chung-Hyun Ro, "Suffering and Hope: An Evaluation of the Consultation," *Reformed World* 36, no. 1 (1980):31.

[4]Leslie Weatherhead, *Why Do Men Suffer?* (New York: Abingdon, 1936), p. 12.

[5]C. S. Lewis, *The Magician's Nephew* (New York: Collier Books, 1955), p. 142.

[6]Ibid., p. 164.

[7]Heschel, *The Prophets*, 1:57.

[8]Quoted in Lehman Strauss, *The Day God Died* (Grand Rapids: Zondervan, 1965), p. 68.

Chapter 7   The Sufferer's Imitation of God

[1]F. J. McConnell, *Is God Limited?* (New York: Abingdon, 1924), p. 293.

[2]J. B. Phillips, *The Church under the Cross* (New York: Macmillan, 1956), p. 22.

[3]Louis Evely, *Suffering* (Garden City, N.Y.: Doubleday, 1967), p. 23.

[4]Jürgen Moltmann, "The Crucified God," *Theology Today*, April 1974, p. 18.

[5]Dietrich Bonhoeffer, *Letters and Papers From Prison* (Huntington, N.Y.: Fontana, 1953), pp. 122-23.

[6]James E. Sellers, *When Trouble Comes: A Christian View of Evil, Sin, and Suffering* (New York: Abingdon, 1960), pp. 102-3.

[7]Evely, p. 24.

[8]Jürgen Moltmann, *The Crucified God* (New York: Harper & Row,

1974), p. 226.

⁹Ibid., p. 49.

¹⁰Lewis B. Smedes, *Love within Limits* (Grand Rapids: Eerdmans, 1978), pp. 2-3.

¹¹Leslie D. Weatherhead, *Salute to a Sufferer* (Nashville: Abingdon, 1962), p. 89.

¹²Frederick W. Farrar, *The Life of Christ* (Dutton, Dovar: Cassell and Co., 1897), p. 440; quoted in, Josh McDowell, *Evidence That Demands a Verdict* (Campus Crusade for Christ, 1972), p. 205.

¹³This story is told in "An Interview with Joni Eareckson," *Eternity* (May 1981), p. 25.

Where is God when I hurt?

Does he sit idly by, unmoved
by my pain or sorrow? Does he merely
philosophize about the good it
will do me? Or does he in some vital
and comforting way enter
into my suffering and take it
upon himself?
Charles Ohlrich confronts
these tough questions in this keen
and sensitive exploration of what
Scripture tells us about the
God who suffers.
Charles Ohlrich holds the B.A. in
biblical studies from Wheaton College,
Wheaton, Illinois.

ISBN 0-87784-376-7   > > $3.25